BROTHER AND SISTER

BROTHER AND SISTER

A Memoir and the Letters

OF

ERNEST AND HENRIETTE RENAN

TRANSLATED BY

LADY MARY LOYD

New York
MACMILLAN AND CO.
AND LONDON
1896

All rights reserved

COPYRIGHT, 1896,
BY MACMILLAN AND CO.

Norwood Press
J. S. Cushing & Co. — Berwick & Smith
Norwood Mass. U.S.A.

NOTE

THE Memoir of Henriette Renan which precedes her correspondence with her brother is the exact reproduction of a pamphlet of which Ernest Renan had a hundred copies printed in September 1862 under the title, "Henriette Renan: A Memorial for those who knew her." In its opening lines the following sentence will attract attention: "These pages are not intended for the general public, and will never be offered to it."

In 1883 Ernest Renan thus expressed himself in the Preface to his "Souvenirs d'Enfance et de Jeunesse":—

"The person who has had most influence on my life — my sister Henriette — scarcely appears in this work of mine. A year after the death of that beloved being, in September 1862, I wrote a little pamphlet, consecrated to her memory, for the benefit of the few who had known her. A hundred copies only were printed. My sister was so modest, her aversion to the bustle of the world was so extreme, that if I had offered these pages to the general public I should have fancied her casting reproaches on me out of her grave. The idea of adding them to this present volume has occasionally occurred to me, and then again I have felt it would be a sort of desecration. The little work has been read with sympathy by a few individuals who were full of kindly feeling towards my sister and myself. But I have no right to expose a memory I hold so sacred to the scornful judgment which is part of the right acquired over a work by purchase. It seemed to me I should do as wrong by the insertion of these pages in a book placed on the open market, as if I exhibited her portrait in an auction room. The pamphlet will not be reprinted, therefore, till after I am dead."

In a codicil to his will, dated November 4, 1888, Ernest Renan thus authorises the present reprint: "My wife will decide the nature of the publicity to be given to my little volume of memorials of my sister Henriette." The reprint now presented was, in fact, prepared by Madame Renan, who is responsible also for the selection of the letters.

MY SISTER HENRIETTE

A MEMOIR

Man's memory is but an imperceptible mark in the furrow each individual leaves on the book of Eternity, yet it is not traced in vain. The human conscience is the highest expression known to us of the summed-up conscience of the Universe. The esteem in which a single man is held forms a part of Absolute Justice. Thus, although lives nobly lived stand in no need of recollection, save by God Himself, some effort is invariably made to fix the image of their memory. I should be all the more to blame were I to leave this duty to my sister Henriette unperformed, because I alone knew all the treasures of that elect soul. Her timidity, her reserve, her fixed opinion that a woman's life should be a hidden one, cast a veil over her rare qualities which few were permitted to lift. Her existence was one succession of acts of devotion, destined to remain unknown. Her secret shall not be betrayed by me. These pages were not written for the public, and will never be offered to it. But those few to whom she revealed her inner self would reproach me did I not endeavour to set forth in order anything that served to complete their recollection of her.

HENRIETTE RENAN

I

My sister Henriette was born at Tréguier on 22nd July 1811. Her existence was saddened early, and absorbed by the sterner duties. She never knew any pleasures save those she drew from the practice of virtue and from her heart's affections. From our father she inherited a melancholy temperament, which left her but little taste for frivolous amusement, and which even inspired her with a certain inclination to shun the world and its delights. She had none of that gay, lively, witty nature which my mother carried even into her vigorous and splendid old age. Her religious feelings, narrowed in their beginnings within the Catholic formula, were always deep in the extreme. Tréguier, the little town where we were born, is an ancient episcopal city, rich in poetic memories. It was one of those great monastic towns, Gallic and Irish at once, built by the Breton emigrants of the sixth century. Its founder was an Abbé Tual or Tugdual. When, in the ninth century, Noménoé, desirous of establishing a Breton nationality, transformed all the great monasteries of the coasts of the Nord into bishoprics, the "Pabre-Tual," or Monastery of St. Tual, was among their number. In the sixteenth and seventeenth centuries Tréguier became a somewhat important ecclesiastical centre, and the gathering-point of a small local nobility. At the Revolution the Bishopric was suppressed, but after the re-establishment of Catholic worship the important Church buildings possessed by the town caused it to rise again into an ecclesiastical centre, a city of convents and religious foundations. Bourgeois life has developed but little within its walls. Its streets, save one or two, are long, deserted alleys, formed by high convent walls or ancient canonical houses, surrounded by their gardens. A general air of distinction strikes you everywhere, and gives the poor dead city a charm unpossessed by the richer and livelier bourgeois towns which have sprung up over the rest of that country.

The cathedral especially, a very fine fourteenth-century edifice, with its tall naves, its astonishingly bold architecture, its graceful, exceedingly high and slender steeple, and its old Roman tower, the remains of some still more ancient building, seemed formed to inspire lofty thoughts. It used to be left open very late at night, so that pious folk might pray there. Lighted by

THE CATHEDRAL — TRÉGUIER

a solitary lamp, in that warm damp atmosphere peculiar to ancient buildings, the huge empty fabric loomed vast and full of terror. The neighbourhood of the town is rich in legends, beautiful or weird. Within a quarter of a league stands the chapel, built close to the birthplace of the good lawyer, St. Ives, the favourite Breton saint of the last century, whom local faith has ended by erecting to the position of defender of the weak and redresser of all wrongs. Near it, on a considerable eminence, is the old Church of St. Michel, long since destroyed by lightning. Thither we were taken on Holy Thursday every year. It is an article of popular belief that on that day, and during the profound silence then imposed on them, all the bells travel to Rome to crave the Papal benediction. We used to climb the ruin-covered hillock to watch them pass, and, closing our eyes, we could *see* them float through the air, bending gently, their robes of lace, the very ones they had worn at their baptismal ceremony, fluttering softly behind them. Somewhat farther on, in a charming valley, rises the little Chapel of the Five Wounds. On the farther side of the river, beside an ancient holy well, is Notre-Dame-du-Tromeur, a spot much venerated by pilgrims.

A childhood passed in these surroundings, full of poetry and dreamy sadness, resulted in my sister's strong inclination towards a life of retirement. Some former nuns, driven from their convent by the Revolution, and who had turned school-teachers, taught her to read and to recite the Psalms in Latin. She learnt everything that is chanted in church by heart, and the attention she later bestowed on the ancient text, comparing it with the French and the Italian, led to her knowing a good deal of Latin, though she never regularly studied it. Nevertheless her education would have necessarily remained very incomplete had not a lucky fate given her an instructress superior to any the neighbourhood had up till then possessed. The noble families of Tréguier had returned from the emigration utterly ruined. A lady belonging to one of these families, who had been educated in England, commenced giving lessons. She was a person of distinction both in tastes and manner. She made a deep impression on my sister, and her recollection of her never grew dim. The misfortunes which surrounded Henriette in early life increased her innate tendency to thoughtfulness. Our paternal grandfather had belonged to a kind of clan of peasant sailors which peoples all the "pays" of Goëlo. Our father served with the fleets of the Republic. After the maritime disasters of those days, he commanded ships on his own account, and by degrees was carried into a considerable trade. This was a great blunder. Absolutely untutored in business matters, simple and incapable of

CLOISTERS OF THE CATHEDRAL—TRÉGUIER

calculation, perpetually checked by that timidity which makes the sailor a very child in practical life, he saw his little family fortune melt gradually away into an abyss he could not fathom. His weak and sensitive nature could not withstand such trials — little by little his grasp on existence weakened. My sister was the hourly spectator of the ravages made by anxiety and misfortune on that good and gentle spirit, strayed into occupations of an order to which he was utterly unfitted. This bitter experience led to her precocious development. By the time she was twelve years old she was grave in thought and appearance, borne down with anxiety, haunted by anxious thoughts and melancholy presentiments. Returning from one of his long voyages in our cold and gloomy seas, my father had one last gleam of happiness — I came into the world in February 1823. The advent of a little brother was a great comfort to my sister. She attached herself to me with all the ardour of a shy and tender nature, endued with an immense longing to love something. I remember yet the petty tyrannies I practised on her, and against which she never revolted. When she was going out in full dress to attend gatherings of girls of her own age, I would cling to her gown and beseech her to remain. Then she would turn back, take off her holiday attire, and stay with me. One day, in joke, she threatened she would die if I was not a good child, and pretended to be dead, in fact, sitting in an arm-chair. The horror caused me by the feigned immobility of my dear sister is perhaps the strongest impression ever made upon me, whom fate did not permit to witness her last sigh. Beside myself, I flew at her, and bit her terribly on the arm. I can hear the shriek she gave even now. To all the reproaches showered on me I could only make one answer, "But why were you dead? Are you going to die again?"

In July 1828 our father's misfortunes culminated in a fearful catastrophe. One day his ship returned from St. Malo into the port of Tréguier without him. The crew, being questioned, declared they had not seen him for several days. For a whole month my mother sought him in indescribable anguish. At last she heard a corpse had been found upon the shore at Erqui, a village lying between St. Brieuc and Cape Fréhel. It proved to be our father's body.

How came he by his death? Was he overtaken by one of those accidents so common in the life of seafaring men? Did he forget himself in one of those long dreams of the Infinite, which, in that Breton race, often verge upon the eternal slumber? Did he feel he had earned repose? Had he seated himself upon the rock, conscious he had struggled enough, and said, "This stone shall be the stone of my eternal rest.

THE HOUSE WHERE ERNEST RENAN WAS BORN

Here will I lie, for I have chosen it!" We know not. He was buried in the sand, where the waves sweep over him twice daily. I have not yet been able to raise a stone which shall testify to the passer-by how much I owe him. My sister's grief was profound. She inherited my father's nature. She had loved him tenderly. Every time she spoke of him it was with tears. She was persuaded his sorely-tried soul stood justified and pure for ever in the sight of God.

II

FROM that day forward poverty was our appointed lot. My brother, then nineteen years of age, departed to Paris, and there entered on that life of labour and constant application which never was to know its full reward. We left Tréguier, which had grown too sad a place of residence for us, and went to live at Lannion, where my mother's family resided. My sister was seventeen years old. Her religious faith had always been lively, and more than once the idea of entering the conventual life had much engaged her thoughts. On winter evenings she would take me to church underneath her own cloak. It was a great delight to me to tread the snow under its all-embracing shelter. But for me she would, without any doubt whatever, have adopted a state of life in evident accordance with her native piety, her lack of fortune, and the customs of her country. Her heart turned specially to the Convent of Ste. Anne at Lannion, which united the care of the sick with that of the education of young girls. Alas! had she but followed her bent, she might have worked more successfully for her own ultimate happiness. But she was too good a daughter and too devoted a sister to prefer her own peace to her duties, even though the religious prejudices which she then shared might have reassured her on that head.

From that time forth she looked upon herself as responsible for my future. Noticing my awkward movements one day, she perceived I was striving shyly to conceal the rents in a worn-out garment. She burst into tears. The sight of the poor child, destined to such black poverty, with instincts so removed therefrom, wrung her heart. She resolved to face the struggle with life, and undertook the task of filling up, by her unaided efforts, the abyss our father's misfortunes had opened at our feet. A young girl's manual labour was quite unequal to such an undertaking. The career she embraced was the bitterest of all others. It was decided that we should return to Tréguier, and that she should there take up the duties of a professional teacher. Of all the conditions of existence open to the choice of a well-educated and undowered person, the education of girls in a small provincial town is, beyond all contradiction, that which demands the greatest courage. The period was that immediately succeeding the Revolution of 1830, an unfortunate and critical moment in those remote provinces. Under the Restoration, the nobility, seeing its privileges were uncontested, had shared frankly in the social movement. Now, in its fancied humiliation, it avenged itself by withdrawing within a narrow circle, and thus impoverished the development of society at large. All Legitimist families made a point of confiding their children to religious communities alone. The middle class, for the sake of being in the fashion, and aping people of quality, soon followed the same custom. My sister—incapable of condescending to those vulgarly-clever methods without which it is well-nigh impossible for a private school to succeed—my sister, with her unusual distinction, her deep earnestness, and her thorough information, saw her little school deserted. The modesty, the reserve, the exquisite tone of mind which she carried into everything she did, were so many causes of her failure in this matter. Struggling with the most paltry touchiness, forced to reckon with the silliest pretensions, her great and noble spirit wore itself out in a hopeless, endless contest with a decadent society, robbed of the best of its former elements by a revolution which had not as yet endowed it with any of its benefits.

Some few people, superior to the local small-mindedness, knew how to value her. An exceedingly intelligent man, free from the prejudices which have reigned supreme in provincial towns since their aristocratic population has either completely disappeared or grown warped in mind and stupidly reactionary, conceived a very deep affection for her. In spite of a birthmark to which it took some time to grow accustomed, my sister was at that age remarkably attractive. Those who only knew her late in life, and worn by a trying climate, cannot fancy the delicacy of her features and their languorous charm in earlier years. Her eyes were peculiarly soft, and her hand the prettiest and daintiest imaginable. Certain proposals were made, coupled with discreetly indicated conditions. The effect of these would, in fact, have been to separate her in a measure from her own people, for whom it was thought she had already toiled sufficiently. She refused them, although the clear-mindedness and justice of her own nature inspired her with a real regard for one in whom she recognised similar qualities. She preferred poverty to affluence unshared by her family. Yet her position was growing more and more distressing. The fees due to her were so irregularly paid, that we now and then regretted having left Lannion, where we had met with far greater kindness and sympathy. Then it was she resolved to drain the bitter cup to its very dregs. A lady friend of the family, who travelled to Paris about this time, spoke to her of a situation as under-mistress in a small school for girls. The poor girl accepted it. At the age of four-and-twenty, friendless, without advisers, she went out into a world which was utterly unknown to her, and in which she was doomed to serve a cruel apprenticeship. The beginning of her Paris life was terrible. That cold and arid world, so full of imposition and imposture, that populous desert, wherein she counted not one single friend, drove her desperate. The deep attachment which we Bretons bear our country, our national habits, and our domestic life, awoke in her with agonising bitterness. Lost in an ocean where her modesty was misunderstood, prevented by her extreme reserve from contracting those kindly acquaintanceships which console and support, even when they do not materially assist us, she fell into a state of nostalgia so profound as to compromise her health. What makes the Breton's condition so cruel in the early days of his transplanting from his home is that he feels forsaken at once by men and by God Himself. The heavens seem darkened to him. His happy belief in the general morality of the universe, his tranquil optimism, are shaken to their foundations. He feels himself cast out of paradise into a hell of icy indifference. The voice of all that is good and beautiful sounds hollow in his ears, and he is tempted to cry out, "How shall I sing the song of the Lord in a strange land?" To crown my sister's misfortunes, the first houses to which she was led by fate were quite unworthy of her. Let the reader imagine a gentle girl, who had never left her God-fearing little town, her mother, and her friends, suddenly planted in the midst of a frivolous-minded school society, where her serious feelings were incessantly wounded, and whose leaders never betrayed any sentiments but such as proved their light-mindedness, indifference, or sordid love of personal interest. Owing to these early experiences she always maintained a very low opinion of the methods of female education in Paris. A score of times she was on the eve of departure, and all her invincible courage was needful to induce her to remain.

But, little by little, people learnt to value her. The management of the studies in a scholastic establishment, a very creditable one, this time was intrusted to her; but the obstacles she encountered to the realisation of her views, owing to the niggardliness inevitable in private institutions, and almost invariably countenanced by the proprietors for the sake of the paltry gain it brings, prevented her ever taking much pleasure in this particular line of teaching. She used to work sixteen hours a day. She passed all the public examinations prescribed by the regulations. This labour did not have the same effect on her mind as it might have on a more mediocre intelligence. Instead of exhausting, it strengthened it, and produced a prodigious mental development. Her information, already very considerable, became exceptional. She made a study of modern history, and in later years a few words of mine would suffice to enable her to seize the sense of the most delicate criticism. Simultaneously her religious ideas underwent modification. From history she learnt the insufficiency of any dogma; but the fundamental religious sentiment, which was hers by nature, as well as by reason of her early education, was too deeply rooted to be shaken. All that development of thought which might have been dangerous in another woman was harmless here, for she kept it in her own heart. The cultivation of the mind had its absolute and intrinsic value in her sight. She never dreamt of turning it into a means of satisfying her vanity. It was in the year 1838 that she brought me to Paris. Educated at Tréguier by some worthy priests who managed a sort of seminary there, I had early given signs of an inclination towards the ecclesiastical state of life. The prizes I won at school delighted my sister, who mentioned them to a kind-hearted and distinguished man, physician to the school in which she taught, and a very zealous Catholic, Dr. Descuret, author of "La Médecine des Passions." He mentioned the chance of getting a good pupil to Monseigneur Dupanloup, then the brilliantly successful manager of the small seminary of "St. Nicholas du Chardonnet," and came back to my sister with the news that he had the offer of a scholarship for me. I was then fifteen and a half years old. My sister, whose own Catholic convictions were beginning to totter, was already inclined to view the very clerical bent of my education with some regret. But she knew the respect due to a child's faith. Never did she breathe one word to dissuade me from a path which I was following of my freest volition. She came to see me every week, still wearing the plain green woollen shawl which had sheltered her proud poverty away in Brittany. She was just the same gentle, loving girl, but with a touch of firmness and wisdom which the trials of life and her severe studies had added to her.

The educational career is such a thankless one for women, that after five years spent in Paris, and several illnesses brought on by over-work, my sister was still far from being able to suffice for all the charges she had taken upon herself. True it is that she took a view of them which would have discouraged any one else. Our father had left debts far exceeding the value of our paternal homestead, the only property remaining to us. But our mother was so beloved, and in those days, in that kindly country, business was still done after so patriarchal a fashion, that no creditor dreamt of pressing for the discharge of our liabilities. It was settled that my mother should keep the house and repay what and when she could. My sister would not listen to any idea of rest till all this old and heavy debt was cleared off. Thus it was that she ended by accepting proposals made her in 1840 to undertake private teaching in Poland. It was a question of years of expatriation and of accepting a state of trying personal dependence. But she had made a far greater effort when she had quitted Brittany to go out into the wide world. She started in January 1841, crossed the Black Forest and the whole of South Germany buried in snow, joined the family she was about to enter at Vienna, and then, crossing the Carpathian range, she reached the Château of Clémensow on the banks of the Bug, a dreary residence, where for ten long years she was to learn how bitter exile is, even when sweetened by a lofty motive.

This time, at all events, fate brought her one compensation for its many former injustices, by placing her in a family which I may mention without hesitation, since a contemporary glory which has brought its name to every lip has added lustre to its historic renown. It was that of Comte André Zamoysky. The passionate eagerness with which she undertook her duties — the affection she conceived for her three pupils — the delight of seeing her efforts bear fruit, especially in the person of her whose youth caused her to remain longest under her care, the Princess

Cécile Lubomirska — the unusual esteem she earned from all the members of this noble family, who never ceased, even after her return to France, to appeal to her sagacity for timely counsel — the close affinity, in their mutual gravity and uprightness, between her own character and that of the household in which she dwelt — all helped her to forget the sadness inseparable from the nature of her position, and the rigours of a climate exceedingly unsuited to her constitution. She grew fond of Poland, and conceived a special feeling of esteem for the Polish peasant, in whom she recognised a good-hearted being, full of lofty religious instincts, not unlike the peasantry of Brittany, but of a less energetic nature. Her travels in Germany and Italy completed the process of ripening her intelligence. She made several and repeated stays at Warsaw, Vienna, and Dresden. Venice and Florence were a perfect dream of delight to her; but Rome especially enthralled her. In that imperial city she grew to see, and that calmly enough, the distinction the philosophic mind must draw between religion in its essence and its specific formula. She loved, with Lord Byron, to call it "dear city of my soul." Like all foreigners who have lived there, she even grew to feel indulgent towards those puerile and senseless details which environ the Papacy in these later days.

III

In 1845 I left the Seminary of St. Sulpice. Thanks to the wise and liberal spirit animating the managers of that establishment, I was far advanced in philological study, and my religious convictions were correspondingly shaken. Here again Henriette was my true helper. She had outstripped me in the path of doubt, and her faith in Catholicism had completely disappeared; but she had always refrained from exercising the slightest influence over me in that respect. When I made known to her the doubts which tormented me, making me feel it a duty to relinquish a career which indispensably demands the most unquestioning faith, she was overjoyed, and offered her aid to support me on the thorny road. I was about entering on life, at the age of twenty-three, old in thought, but as inexperienced, as ignorant of the world as a young man well could be. I literally did not know a soul; I lacked the assurance of an ordinary boy of fifteen. I had not even taken my degree of *bachelier ès lettres*. We agreed that I should seek for some employment in a school in Paris of the nature known as *au pair*, which would, that is to say, give me board and lodging, leaving me considerable leisure for my studies. My sister advanced me a sum of twelve hundred francs (forty-four pounds), to enable me to wait, and supplement whatever insufficiency of income such a position might at first present.

That sum was the corner-stone of my whole life. I never exhausted it, but it secured me the calm of mind so indispensable if I was to think in peace, and saved me from being overwhelmed by taskwork which would have broken me down. At this crucial moment in my life, Henriette's beautiful letters were my support and consolation. While I was struggling with difficulties increased by my total inexperience of the world, her health was suffering severely from the severity of the Polish winters; a chronic affection of the larynx developed, and in 1850 took so serious a form that her return was deemed necessary. Her task, moreover, was accomplished; our father's liabilities had been completely discharged; the small property he had left us was safe in my mother's hands, freed from all debt, and my brother's work had earned him a position which promised to become a wealthy one. The idea of a meeting occurred to both of us. I joined her in Berlin in September 1850. Those ten years of exile had utterly transformed her.

Premature old age had wrinkled her brow. Of the charms she still possessed when she bade me farewell in the parlour of the Seminary of St. Nicholas, naught remained save her delightful expression of ineffable goodness.

Then began those happy years, the recollection of which still draws tears from my eyes.

We hired a small apartment at the bottom of a garden near the Val de Grâce. Here we enjoyed the most perfect solitude. She had no relations with the outer world, and desired none. Our windows looked over the garden of the Carmelite nuns in the Rue de l'Enfer. The life led by these recluses gave, in a measure, the pattern of her own, and was her only interest during the long hours I was absent at the Bibliothèque Nationale. She had the extremest respect for my work; I have known her sit of an evening for hours by my side, holding her breath lest she should disturb me. Yet she liked to see me, and the door between our two rooms was always open. So judicious and so ripened had her affection for me grown, that the secret communion of our thoughts sufficed her. Naturally exacting and jealous-hearted, she was satisfied with but a few minutes each day, so long as she felt assured she was the sole object of my affection. Thanks to her vigorous economy, she managed my home on exceedingly limited means, so that nothing ever lacked, and even endued it with a simple charm of its own. So perfect was the union of our minds that we scarcely needed to communicate our thoughts. Our general views concerning the universe and the deity were identical. There was not a delicate shade in the theories I was then evolving which she did not appreciate. She surpassed me in knowledge on many points of modern history, which she had studied at the fountain-head. The general plan of my career, the scheme of inflexible sincerity I had mapped out, was so essentially the combined product of our two consciences, that, had I been tempted to fail in any particular of it, she, like a second self, would have been found beside me to call me back to duty. Thus her influence in my mental sphere was very great. She was my incomparable amanuensis. She copied all my works, and understood them so thoroughly that I could trust to her as to the living index of my own intelligence. In the matter of form I owe her an immensity. She read everything I wrote in the proofs, and her invaluable criticism would discover delicate shades of negligence in style which might otherwise have escaped me. She had formed an admirable one of her own, modelled on the classics, so severely correct that I doubt whether, since the days of Port Royal, any writer has ever set himself a loftier ideal of perfect diction. This made her a very severe critic. She favoured but few of our contemporary writers, and when she saw the essays I had composed before our reunion, and which had not had time to reach her in Poland, she was only half contented with them. She shared the tendency of their ideas, and she felt, at all events, that the measured exposition of deep thoughts of such an order should be expressed by each person with perfect freedom of individual speech; but she thought their form abrupt and careless. Some passages in them struck her as being exaggerated, harsh in tone, and as treating our language after a fashion which was barely respectful.

She convinced me that everything may be clearly expressed in the simple and correct style of the best authors, and that novel forms and violent imagery always denote either misplaced pretension or ignorance of the writer's real resources. Thus a fundamental change in my own style dates from this period. I formed a habit of composing with an eye to her remarks, writing various passages to see what effect they would produce on her, and resolved to sacrifice them should she demand it.

Since I lost her, this habit of my mind has grown to be a semblance of the anguish of a patient who has suffered amputation, and who has the limb he was deprived of constantly within his sight. She was a radical factor in my intellectual existence, and with her a part of my actual being passed away. On all philosophical subjects we had grown to see with the same eyes and feel as with one heart. She so thoroughly comprehended my method of thought that she almost always anticipated what I was about to say, the idea striking us both at the same moment. But on one point she far surpassed me. While I still sought, in matters of the soul, for interesting controversy or artistic study, nothing ever tarnished the purity of her close communion with Good. Her religious worship of the truth suffered not the smallest note of discord. One quality of my work which gave her pain was the sarcastic spirit which possessed me, and which I was apt to carry into my best work. Never having known real suffering, I took the cautious smile which human vanity or weakness will provoke to be a sort of token of my philosophy. This habit of mine distressed her, and I relinquished it little by little for her sake. I now see how right she was. Good men should be simply good. Every touch of sarcasm implies some residuum of vanity and personal defiance, which in the long-run surely degenerates into want of taste.

Her religion had reached the acme of simplicity. She absolutely rejected the supernatural, but she preserved the deepest attachment to the Christian practice. It was not Protestantism exactly, even in its broadest sense, which attracted her. She had the tenderest recollection of Catholicism, of the chanting, and Psalms, and pious practices amid which her childhood had been spent. She was a saint minus the saint's precise faith in religious symbolism and its narrow observances.

About a month before her death we had a religious conversation with that excellent man Dr. Gaillardot on the terrace of our house at Ghazir. She would fain have checked my strong inclination towards the formulated conception of an impersonal Deity and a purely ideal immortality. Without being what is vulgarly called a Deist, she could not tolerate the thought of reducing religion to a mere abstract idea. In practice, at all events, all was clear to her. "Yes," she said, "when my last hour comes, I shall have the consolation of telling myself I have done all the good I could. If there is a thought on earth which is not vanity, that is one."

A keen appreciation of Nature was the source of some of her most exquisite pleasures. A fine day, a sunbeam, a flower, would suffice to delight her. She had a perfect comprehension of the delicate art of the great Italian idealist schools, but she could find no pleasure in that brutal or violent style which seeks for something else than beauty.

A special circumstance gave her an unusual acquaintance with the history of the Art of the Middle Ages. She it was who collected for me all the notes for the paper on the condition of the Fine Arts in the fourteenth century which will be incorporated in the twenty-fourth volume of the "Histoire Littéraire de France." For this purpose, and with the most admirable patience and care, she examined every great archæological work published during the last half-century, and collected every item that could serve our purpose. Her own conclusions, which she noted down at the same time, were remarkable for their accuracy, and I almost invariably had to adopt them in the end. To complete our researches, we travelled together into the country which was the cradle of Gothic art, the Vexin, the Valois, and the Beauvois regions, and the localities lying round Noyon, Laon, and Rheims. During all this inquiry, in which she took the deepest interest, she displayed extraordinary activity. The ideal life to her was one of labour and retirement lapped in affection. Often she would repeat those words of Thomas à Kempis, "In angello cum libello." Amid such peaceful avocations many happy hours were spent, her mind perfectly tranquil, and her heart, generally so anxious, in deepest repose. Her power of work was prodigious. I have known her never quit her self-imposed task from morning till night for days together. She assisted in editing several educational journals, one managed by her friend Mdlle. Ulliac-Trémadeure in particular. She never signed her articles, and such was her modesty that she gave herself no opportunity of gaining anything beyond the esteem of a small minority. But indeed the vile taste prevailing in the composition of all French works intended for the purposes of female education prevented her ever looking for great pecuniary remuneration or success. This work was undertaken more especially to oblige her friend, who had grown old and infirm. It was in her letters that her whole being revealed itself. Her travelling journals, too, were excellent. I had looked to her to relate the unscientific details of our journey in the East. Alas! the history of that aspect of my enterprise, which I had confided to her care, has perished with her. The fragment I have discovered among her papers is excellent. We hope to publish it, and complete what is lacking with her letters. Later on we shall bring out a description written by her of the great maritime expeditions of the fifteenth and sixteenth centuries. She had studied deeply for the purpose of this work, and had brought a critical acumen to bear upon it rarely found in books intended for the young. She never did anything by halves. Her fine taste for absolute truthfulness proved the accuracy of her judgment.

She was not witty, if that word is taken, in the French acceptation, to mean something light and bantering—she never made game of any living being. She hated all malice, and thought it cruelty. I remember once, at a *pardon* in Lower Brittany, to which we went by water, our boat was preceded by one filled with poor ladies, who, in their desire to be smart for the occasion, had indulged in a style of toilet decoration at once paltry and tasteless. Our companions laughed at them, and the poor ladies perceived it. I saw her burst into tears. To her it seemed barbarous cruelty to make a mock of harmless beings who were forgetting their troubles in a day's pleasuring, and who perhaps had pinched themselves sorely out of deference to public opinion. A person who attracted ridicule at once acquired her pity. With pity she gave love, and set herself between the mocker and his prey.

Hence arose her indifference to society, and her lack of that ordinary conversation which is almost invariably a tissue of ill-nature and frivolity. She had grown old before her time, and she had a habit of exaggerating her age, both in her dress and manner. She had a sort of worship for sorrow. She welcomed, she almost cultivated, every opportunity of shedding tears. Grief became an enduring and almost an enjoyable sensation with her. Middle-class people, as a rule, misunderstood her, and thought her stiff and embarrassed in manner. Nothing which was not completely good in its way found favour in her eyes. She could not be false to her own self. The lower orders and peasants, on the contrary, found her exquisitely kind, and those who knew how to touch the finest chords of her nature soon learnt to appreciate its depth and its distinction.

She had charming womanly flashes now and then. Her youth would return to her for the nonce; she would seem to smile at life, and the veil that parted her from the outer world would drop.

These passing moments of enchanting weakness, fleeting gleams of a dawn long past, were full of melancholy tenderness. She was far superior in this particular to those persons who profess the indifference preached by the Mystic school in all its gloomy abstraction. She loved life, she was full of good taste, she could smile over a jewel or some womanly trifle as she would smile upon a flower. She had never pronounced the ascetic Christian's sweeping renunciation of Nature. Virtue, in her eyes, was an austere endeavour, a deliberate effort, the natural instinct of a pure soul, tending in spontaneous striving towards good, serving God without fear or trembling.

Thus for six years we lived a very pure and elevated life. My position was always a very modest one, but that was her own desire. Even had I thought of it, she would not have permitted me to sacrifice one tittle of my independence to my worldly advancement. The unexpected disasters which befell our brother, and led to the loss of all our savings, did not dismay her. She would have gone abroad again, had that been necessary to ensure the steady development of my literary life. Oh! my God, have I done all that in me lay to ensure her happiness? With what bitterness do I now reproach myself for my habit of reserve towards her, for not having told her oftener how dear I held her, for having yielded too easily to my love of silent meditation, for not having made the most of every hour in which she was spared to me! But I take that rare soul to witness that she was always in my heart of hearts, that she ruled my whole moral life as none other ever ruled, that she was the constant beginning and end of all my existence, in sorrow and in joy. If I failed her, it was by a certain stiffness of manner which should never give pause to those who know me well, and by a feeling of respect, misplaced perhaps, which caused me instinctively to avoid anything resembling a desecration of her holiness. A similar feeling checked her in her intercourse with me. My lengthened clerical education, one of absolute seclusion during four years, had given me a habit of mind in this respect which her inherent and delicate reserve prevented her opposing as much as she might have done perhaps.

IV

My inexperience of life, and my ignorance, especially of the profound difference between the male and female heart, led me to ask a sacrifice of her, which would have been beyond the powers of any other woman. I had too deep a feeling of what I owed to such a friend to dream of changing our manner of life in any way without her approbation. But she herself, with her usual great-heartedness, took the first step. In the earliest days after we met again, she strongly recommended me to marry. She frequently recurred to the subject; she even mentioned to one of our friends, unknown to me, a marriage she had planned for me, and which had come to nothing. The initiative she thus displayed led me into an absolute mistake. I sincerely believed it would cause her no pain were I to tell her I had fixed my choice upon a person worthy to share my home with her. I had always taken for granted she would ever remain what she had hitherto been to me, an accomplished and beloved sister, incapable of giving or taking offence, sure enough of the feeling I had for her not to be wounded by that with which another person might inspire me. I now see how mistaken such an idea was. A woman's love differs from a man's. All her affections are jealous and exclusive. She admits no shade of difference betwixt divers kinds of affection. But some excuse I had. I was misled by my own extreme simplicity, and to some extent also by my sister herself. To tell the truth, I believe she was the dupe of her own brave heart. When the marriage she had planned for me fell through, she was sorry after a fashion, although in some respects the idea had ceased to tempt her. But so mysterious is the heart of woman, that the trial she had herself gone out smilingly to meet seemed cruel when it came to her. She was ready and willing to drink the bitter cup her own hands had prepared, but she shrunk from that I offered her, though I had used all my art to make it sweet. Such is the terrible result of exaggerated delicacy of sentiment. A brother and sister united by the closest affection, just for lack of sufficient plain-speaking, came to lay snares for each other in all unconsciousness, to seek and fail to find each other in the dark.

Those were bitter days to us. We were tossed by every tempest loving hearts can know. When she told me she had only suggested my marrying, in the first instance, in the desire of trying my affection for herself, when she warned me that the instant of my union with another person would be that of her own departure, my heart stood still. Do I imply that this was the real feeling actuating her, that she actually desired to raise obstacles in the way of the marriage I longed for? No! in good truth. 'Twas but the whirlwind in her passionate soul, the revolt of a heart whose love was strong to violence. The moment she and Mdlle. Cornélie Scheffer met, they conceived that mutual affection which later was so dear to both of them. M. Ary Scheffer's open and noble manner struck and enraptured her. She saw middle-class meanness and paltry touchiness had no place there. Her goodwill was aroused, and yet, at the decisive moment, the woman in her woke again. Her power for goodwill left her.

At last the day dawned which was to end this cruel suffering. Driven into choosing between two affections, I sacrificed everything to the older — that which verged most closely on a duty. I told Mdlle. Scheffer that I could never see her again until my sister's heart ceased to bleed at the thought of our meetings. This took place in the evening. I went home and told my sister what I had done. A great revulsion swept over her soul. The thought of having prevented a union so much desired by me filled her with bitterest remorse. Very early next morning she hastened to M. Scheffer's house, and spent long hours mingling her tears with those of my intended bride. They parted cheerfully and in firm friendship. After my marriage indeed, as before it, we had all things in common. It was her savings which rendered the young housekeeping a possibility. Without her I could never have coped with my new responsibilities. But so confident was I in her goodness that I only long afterwards recognised the ingenuousness of my own behaviour. These alternations in her moods went on for a considerable time. Again and again the cruel overmastering demons of over-anxious tenderness, of jealousy and sudden heart rebellion and swift regrets awoke, and tortured her. Often her melancholy talk would hint at severing her own existence from one which in her gloomiest hours she would assert no longer stood in need of her. But such moments were but as the remnant of some evil dream, which gradually disappears. The delicate tact and feeling of the sister I had given her won the completest victory. When for a passing moment she would blame me, Cornélie's gentle intervention, her simple gaiety and charm, would change our tears to laughter, and we ended the matter in a mutual embrace. The uprightness in heart and feeling manifested by those two women, grappling with the most delicate of all the problems of the affections, were my perpetual admiration. I came to bless the sufferings which had earned me such a happy reconciliation. The ingenuous hope I had indulged of seeing another besides myself complete my sister's happiness, and bring into her existence a gaiety and stir I personally did not know how to supply, was occasionally realised. More fortunate than my indiscretion warranted, I saw my imprudence turn to wisdom, and enjoyed the fruits of my own foolhardiness.

The birth of my little son Ary completed the work of my sister's consolation. Her love for that child was a downright worship. The maternal instinct, with which she overflowed, there found its natural outlet. Her gentleness, her unalterable patience, her love for everything good and simple, made her unspeakably tender to childhood. It was a sort of religion with her, and one which, to her melancholy nature, had an infinite charm. When my second child, a girl, whom we lost in a few months, came into the world, Henriette told me, several times over, that the little one had come to take her own place beside me. She loved the thought of death, and would recur to it with delight.

"You will see, my dear ones," she would say, "the

little flower we have lost will leave a sweet perfume with us." And the memory of the little creature who had gone was long held sacred by her. Sharing as she thus did, with the full strength of her great power of feeling, in all our joys and sorrows, she ended by completely identifying herself with the new life I had brought about her. I count the fact of having realised this masterpiece of self-sacrifice and simple devotion in the person of those two women, whose lives fate linked with mine, as one of the greatest moral satisfactions I have known. They loved each other with a very deep affection, and I have the consolation at this moment of feeling the sorrow that walks beside me is as heavy as my own. Each had her own separate place in my existence, and that without division or exclusion. Each, after her own fashion, was everything to me.

When, a few days before her death, my sister had a kind of presentiment of her approaching end, she spoke some words to me which proved that all her wounds were healed, and that nothing but a memory of the bitterness of bygone days remained.

V

In the year 1860, when the Emperor offered me a scientific mission to the country known in ancient times as Phœnicia, my sister was one of those who pressed me most strongly to accept. In politics she was a sturdy Liberal, but she held that all party feeling should be set aside when it came to realising a plan which in itself promised good fruit, though its sole probable reward was the peril encountered in its execution. It was settled from the first that she should bear me company. Accustomed as I had grown to her personal care and her invaluable collaboration in all my work, I also needed her in this case to manage the expenditure and keep the accounts of the expedition. This duty she performed with the minutest care, and I was able, thanks to her assistance, to carry on a very complicated undertaking during a period extending over a whole year, without ever being disturbed for a single moment by material questions. Her activity was the wonder of all who saw it. Without her help I certainly could not have carried through my self-imposed task — too elaborate a one, perhaps — within so short a space of time. She never left my side. Step by step she followed me up the steepest slopes of Lebanon and across the wilderness of Jordan, seeing everything I saw myself. If I had died, she could have told the story of my travels almost as well as I could have related it myself. The terrible mountain tracks, the privation inevitable in this sort of exploring expedition, never checked her. A thousand times I felt my heart tremble as I watched her swaying on the edge of some precipice. Her steadiness and endurance on horseback were surprising. She would do eight and ten hours' journey in the day. Her health, naturally somewhat frail, withstood the strain by dint of her strong will. But her whole nervous system began to develop an excited condition, symptoms of which appeared in the shape of violent attacks of neuralgia. Twice or thrice, in the midst of the wilderness, she fell into a state of suffering which terrified us. Her astonishing courage deceived us all. So passionately had she identified herself with this investigation of mine, that she was resolved nothing should part her from me till it was accomplished. And the journey in itself was a source of keen enjoyment to her. This year, in fact, was the only one in her life which brought her no actual sorrow, and it was almost the only real reward she ever knew. Her power of fresh enjoyment was complete. She took a childlike delight in all the wonders our new existence revealed to her. Nothing can exceed the charm of spring and autumn in Syria. The perfumed atmosphere seems to inspire every living thing with its own buoyancy. The most exquisite flowers, magnificent cyclamens especially, tuft every rocky crevice, and on the plains lying towards Amrit and Tortosa the horses' feet trample a thick carpet formed of our loveliest garden blossoms. The torrents flowing down the mountain-sides contrast deliciously with the merciless sun that beats upon them.

Our first halt was at the village of Amschit, three-quarters of an hour's ride from Gebeil (Byblos), founded some five-and-twenty or thirty years before by the rich Maronite chief, Mikhaël Tobia. Zakhia, Mikhaël's heir, rendered our stay exceedingly agreeable. He gave us a pretty house overlooking Byblos and the sea. The gentle manners of the people, their invariable civility, the regard they formed for us, and for her in particular, touched us deeply. She was always glad to return to this village, and we made it in some degree our headquarters while in the Byblos region. The village of Sarba, near Djouni, the residence of a kind and worthy family of the name of Khadra, well known to all French travellers in this part of the East, also became a favourite stopping-place with her. She delighted in the lovely Bay of Kesrouan, with its closely dotted villages, its convents perched on every peak, and its mountains running sheer down into the transparent waves. A hymn of delight seemed to rise out of her soul every time this lovely panorama burst upon us as we came out amongst the rocks towards the north on our way down from Gebeil. She grew much attached to the Maronite people generally. A visit she paid to the convent at Bkerké, where the Patriarch then resided, surrounded by bishops whose habits were of a truly Arcadian simplicity, left a very pleasant impression on her memory. She conceived the greatest dislike, on the other hand, to the small European tittle-tattle of Beyrout society, and to the stiffness of that in such towns as Saïda, where the Mussulman type of life predominated. The wonderful sights she witnessed at Tyre delighted her. She was literally rocked by the tempest in the lofty summer-house where she was lodged. The nomad life, always so fascinating in the long-run, had taken hold upon her. Night after night my wife invented some fresh pretext to prevent her staying in her tent alone. She would yield, though always with something of a struggle. She delighted in the atmosphere of close familiarity, shared with those she loved, amidst that spreading wilderness of space.

THE HOUSE AT AMSCHIT

But her most passionate interest was claimed by our journey in Palestine. Jerusalem, with its unrivalled memories, Naplousa and its lovely valley, Mount Carmel, carpeted with spring flowers, and Galilee above all — that earthly paradise laid waste, on which the Divine breath lingers yet, held her spellbound for six enchanted weeks.

Starting from Tyre and from Oum-el-Awamid, we had already made several little expeditions, lasting six or eight days each, into those ancient possessions of the tribes of Asher and Naphtali, where such mighty things were once accomplished. When I first showed her from Kasyoun, above Lake Huleh, the whole region of the Upper Jordan, with the basin of the Lake of Gennesaret, the cradle of the Christian faith, far away in the distance, she thanked me, telling me that sight had been the most precious joy her life had known. Far above that narrow sentiment which attaches historical interest to particular localities, to concrete objects, almost invariably apocryphal in their origin, she always looked for the spirit, the true sense, the general impression left by the event. Our long tours in that splendid country, with Mount Hermon ever in our view, its gorges marked in snowy lines against the azure heavens, haunt the memory like dreams of some other world.

In the month of July, my wife, who had been

with us since January, was obliged to leave us at the call of other duties. The excavations were all finished, the French army had evacuated Syria. We two stayed behind to superintend the removal of the objects unearthed, to complete our exploration of the Upper Lebanon, and to make preparation for a final campaign in Cyprus during the following autumn. Bitterly do I now deplore the share I took in thus prolonging our stay over the months most unhealthful to Europeans residing in Syria. Our last journey in the Lebanon tried my sister very much. We spent three days at Maschnaka, above the Adonis river, sheltered by a mud hut. The perpetual change from chilly valleys to burning rocks, the bad food, the necessity of spending the nights in low-built houses, where one had either to keep every aperture open or to stifle, laid the seeds of that nerve pain which was so soon to make itself apparent. Leaving the deep valleys of Tannourin, after having spent the night at the Convent of Mar-Yakoub, on one of the abruptest crags in that vicinity, we entered the scorching region of Toula. The sudden change overwhelmed us. Towards eleven o'clock, in the village of Helta, she was seized with agonising pain. I made her rest in the village priest's poor hovel, and a little farther on the road, while I was collecting some inscriptions, she tried to snatch some sleep within an oratory. But the native women would not let her rest; they kept coming to look at her and touch her. At last we got to Toula. There two days passed in hideous suffering. We were without succour of any kind, and the untutored roughness of the inhabitants increased her anguish. Never having beheld a European, they swarmed into the house, tormenting her after the most unendurable fashion while I was away prosecuting my researches. As soon as she could sit on horseback, we went as far as Amschit, where she got a little better. But her left eye was affected, and at times she suffered from diplopia.

The intense heat prevailing all along the coast, and our own fatigued condition, made me resolve on settling down at Ghazir, very high above the sea, at the far end of the Bay of Kesrouan. We took leave of the worthy denizens of Amschit and Gebeil. The sun was setting when we reached the mouth of the Adonis river. There we rested for a while. Though far from free of pain, the delicious calm of that beautiful spot fell upon her spirit, and she had an interval of quiet cheerfulness. We climbed the mountain of Ghazir in the moonlight; she was in great delight, and as we left the burning seashore we fancied all the suffering we had known there had departed from us.

Certainly Ghazir is one of the loveliest spots in

the whole world. The valleys around are exquisitely green, and the slopes of Aramoun, a little above it, are more beautiful than anything I saw in the Lebanon. But the inhabitants, corrupted by their commerce with the so-called aristocratic families of that region, have none of the good qualities usually found amongst the Maronites.

We secured a nice little house with a pretty arbour. Within its walls we enjoyed a few days of most delightful rest. We were able to get snow from the crevasses of the upper mountain. Our poor fellow-travellers, her Arab mare and my mule Sada, cropped the herbage close to us. She suffered much during that first fortnight, then the pain quieted down, and God granted her a few more days of perfect happiness before she left this world.

The memory of those days is inexpressibly precious to me. The unavoidable delay connected with such work as we were occupied in winding up left me much leisure. I resolved to note down all the thoughts concerning the life of Jesus which had been stirring in my brain since my sojourn in the Tyrian country and my journey into Palestine. The personality of that great Founder had risen very clearly to my mind as I perused the Gospels in Galilee itself. Buried in the deepest conceivable retirement, with the help of the Gospels and of Josephus, I wrote a "Life of Jesus," carrying the story while I was at Ghazir as far as the last journey to Jerusalem. Exquisite hours, departed all too quickly! I pray eternity may be as sweet! From morning till night I lived intoxicated, as it were, with the idea unfolding itself before my mental vision. I fell asleep pursuing it, and the first ray of sun shooting above the mountain revealed it to me yet clearer, stronger, than before. Henriette was the daily confidant of the progress of my labour. As fast as I could write a page she copied it. "I shall love this book," she said, "because we have done it together, first of all, and then because I like it in itself."

The elevation of her thoughts had never struck me more. In the evening we used to walk on our terrace under the stars. Then she would give me the result of her reflections, full of tact and wisdom. Some of them were absolute revelations to me. She was perfectly happy, and this was certainly the most blessed moment in her life. Our intellectual and moral communion had never been so intimate. She repeatedly told me those days had been a paradise to her. A gentle mournfulness of tone pervaded everything she said. Her physical suffering was only numbed, and would wake, now and again, as though in sinister warning. Then she would complain that fate was miserly, and grudged her the few hours of perfect bliss it had ever granted her.

Early in September Ghazir became a very inconvenient place of residence for me, in view of the fact that the exigencies of my mission called me to Beyrout. We reluctantly bade farewell to our village home, and for the last time passed down that beautiful road beside the river of the Dog, which had grown so familiar to us during the year just gone by. Though the heat was very great, we spent some pleasant hours at Beyrout. The days were exhausting, but the nights delicious, and the sight of Sannin bathed in heavenly glory by the rays of the setting sun was a nightly feast to our delighted eyes. My transport operations were well-nigh concluded. The Cyprus journey was all that remained for me to do. We began to talk of our return to France. Already we dreamt of pale and gentle sunshine, of the cool damp Northern autumn, of the fresh green meadows beside the river Oise, which we had trodden at the same season two years previously. She would dwell with delight on the joy of clasping our little Ary and our aged mother to her heart once more. Now and then she had hours of sadness, in which all her memories of bygone days seemed inextricably mingled; at such moments she would talk about my father, and dwell upon that good and kindly nature, so rich in deep and tender feeling. Her mood had never struck me as more noble and more winning.

On Sunday, September 15th, Admiral de Barbier de Tinan informed me that the crew of the *Caton* could spare a week for a fresh effort to exhume two great sarcophagi at Gebeil, the removal of which had at first been deemed impossible. My presence at Gebeil during that week was really not indispensable. It would have quite sufficed if I had gone there with the *Caton* to furnish certain local information, and then returned overland to Beyrout. But I knew how much she dreaded separations of this kind. And remembering she had enjoyed her former stay at Amschit, a different plan occurred to me — that we should both sail on the *Caton*, spend the week at Amschit and return in the same manner.

So on the Monday we set out. She had been rather unwell the previous day, but the sea passage revived her. She greatly enjoyed the view of the Lebanon in all its summer glory, and while I went with the captain to settle all the details concerning the removal of the sarcophagi, she rested pleasantly on board the ship. In the evening, after the sun had set, we went up to Amschit. Our good friends there, who had never expected to see us again, gave us the heartiest of welcomes, which delighted her. We spent part of the night, after we had dined, on the terrace of Zakhia's house. The sky looked beautiful, and I reminded her of that passage in the Book of Job wherein the aged patriarch boasts as a sign of rare merit — "That his mouth had never kissed his hand, nor his heart been secretly enticed, when he beheld the sun when it shined, or the moon walking in brightness." The whole spirit of the ancient Syrian worship seemed to rise up before us. Byblos lay at our feet; southward, in the sacred region of the Lebanon, rose the strangely jagged outline of the rocks and forest of Djebel-Mousa, which legend denotes as the spot where Adonis perished; the sea, curving away to the north, towards Botrys, seemed to hem us in on either side. That was the last day of perfect happiness in my life. Any future joy that I may know must carry me back to my past, and recall the memory of her who cannot share my present.

On the Tuesday she was less well; and yet I was not alarmed. Her indisposition seemed a mere nothing compared with what I had seen her suffer. I had set to work again, with passionate eagerness, on my "Life of Jesus." We worked all day, and in the evening she continued in good spirits as we sat on the terrace. On Wednesday the suffering increased, and I took upon me to ask the ship's surgeon to visit her. He gave me no reason for anxiety.

On the Thursday her state was just the same. But that day was a fatal one to us, for I was struck down by sickness in my turn. I had carried my mission to its conclusion without any serious illness, and, by a fell chance, the memory of which will haunt me like a nightmare till my life's end, the one moment at which I was to fail was that in which I might have watched over her last agony. On that Thursday morning I had to go down to the anchorage at Gebeil to confer with the captain. Climbing back to Amschit, I felt the sun, reverberating from the scorching rocks upon the hill, had struck me. During the afternoon I had a violent attack of fever, accompanied by sharp neuralgic pains. My sickness was really of the same nature as that which was killing my poor sister. Clever as the doctor of the *Caton* was, he did not recognise it. The pernicious fevers of the Syrian coast present characteristics which none but medical men who have lived in the country can understand. Powerful doses of sulphate of quinine might have saved us both, even at that point. In the evening I felt my senses going. I warned the doctor, who, blind as he was to the nature of our complaint, attached no importance to the fact, and left us. Then, like a terrible vision, arose the fear of what within three days became a dread reality. I shivered at the thought of the risks that threatened us should we fall, alone and unconscious, into the hands of these worthy folk, utterly devoid of intelligence, and with the crudest ideas of medical care. I bade farewell to life with a feeling of extremest bitterness. The loss of my papers, of my "Life of Jesus" in particular, appeared to me utterly inevitable. We had a terrible night; but my poor sister's seems to have been less bad than mine, for I remember her having the strength to say to me next morning, "Your whole night was one long moan."

The Friday, Saturday, and Sunday are like the phases of a painful dream to me. The attack which so nearly carried me off on the Monday had a sort of retroactive effect, almost completely effacing my recollection of the three preceding days. The doctor, most unluckily for us, always saw us in our easier moments, and thus did not foresee the impending crisis. I still worked, but I felt I was working badly. I had reached the episode of the Last Supper in the story of the Passion. When I read the lines over later on, they struck me as being full of a sort of mysterious sense of agitation. My mind had been revolving in a perpetual circle, beating wildly like the shaft of an engine out of gear. Various other particulars still abide with me. I wrote to ask the Sisters of Charity at Beyrout to send me quinine wine, which nobody else in Syria knew how to make, but I was conscious my letter was incoherent. Neither Henriette nor I appear to have had a very clear conception of the gravity of our illness. I settled to depart for France on the ensuing Thursday. "Yes, yes, let us start," she said, with perfect confidence. "Poor me!" she added another time, "I feel I am going to have a great deal of suffering." On one of those two days she was still able, towards sunset, to move out of one chamber into the next. She lay down on a couch in the room I slept and generally worked in. The jalousies were open, and our eyes fell on Djebel-Mousa. She had a momentary presentiment of the end, though not of such a closely approaching one. Her eyes were wet with tears. Her pale face, worn with suffering, regained a little colour as together we looked back sadly and tenderly over her past life. "I will make my will," she said. "You shall be my heir; I have not much to leave; still there is something. I want you to spend my savings in building a family tomb. We must all be gathered together, and lie close side by side. Little Ernestine, too, must be brought back to us." Then she made a mental calculation, pointing with her finger to indicate the interior arrangement of the vault, and seemed to desire it should be large enough for twelve people. She wept as she spoke of little Ary and of our old mother. She told me what I was to give her niece. She pondered over something which would please Cornélie, and pitched on a little Italian book, the "Fioretti" of St. Francis, which had been given to her by M. Berthelot. "I have loved you very dearly," she added then; "sometimes my love has caused you pain. I have been unjust, exclusive; but I have loved you as people do not love now-a-days, as one has no right to love, perhaps." I burst into tears. I spoke of our return home. I led her mind back to little Ary, knowing how closely that thought touched her. She loved to dwell on it, and on every incident connected with her tenderest feelings. She returned again to the beloved memory of our father. That was the last gleam of light we had. We were both of us in the interval between two attacks of fever. Her last was coming in a very few hours. Except for the doctor's short visits we were quite alone, at the mercy of our Arab servants and the villagers; all the other members of the mission had started homewards or were busy elsewhere. I have but little distinct recollection of that fatal Sunday, or I should rather say that others have revived the memories of which every trace had been obliterated. All day long I went on like an automaton to which some outside impulse has been given. I can still distinctly recollect the impression made on me by seeing the peasants going to Mass. Generally, when they knew we were going too, they would gather around to do us honour. The doctor came during the morning. It was settled that the sailors should come up early next day before dawn with a cot for my sister, and that the *Caton* should take us back at once to Beyrout. Towards mid-day I must have worked again in my poor sister's room, for I was told afterwards that my books and notes were found upon her floor, scattered about the mat on which I usually sat. In the afternoon she grew much worse. I wrote to the doctor to hasten up at once, telling him her heart seemed threatened. I do not remember writing the letter, and when it was shown me some days later, it woke no recollection in me. Yet I was able to move about, for our servant, Antoun, told me I had my sister moved into the sitting-room which served as my bed-chamber — that I helped to carry her, and remained with her a considerable time.

We may have bidden each other farewell for all I know. She may have spoken some precious parting word which the terrible hand of fate has wiped from the tablet of my brain. Antoun assured me she never was aware that she was dying, but he was so stupid, and knew so little French, that he may not have realised what passed between us.

The doctor came at six o'clock, the captain with him. Both of them deemed it impossible to think of moving my sister to Beyrout next day. By a strange chance my attack came on while they were with us. I lost consciousness in the captain's arms. The two gentlemen, both of them wise and upright men, though mistaken up till that moment as to the serious nature of our case, took counsel together. The doctor, straightforwardly admitting his own inability to treat an illness the progress of which had escaped his control, requested the captain to go down to Beyrout and return at once with fresh medical assistance. The captain acted on this suggestion. Only, with a respect for Turkish pratique which other navies do not observe even in less urgent cases, he did not start till four o'clock in the morning. By six o'clock he was at Beyrout, and had acquainted Admiral Paris with our condition. With his usual extreme courtesy the admiral ordered him to start back as soon as he had shipped Dr. Louvel, the chief surgeon to the squadron, and Dr. Suquet, the French sanitary officer at Beyrout, who has earned a world-wide reputation, exceeding that of any other Frenchman, by his profound study of Syrian fevers. By half-past ten all these gentlemen were at Amschit. Almost at the same moment Dr. Gaillardot arrived, coming overland. Since the previous evening we had both been lying unconscious, opposite each other, in Zakhia's big sitting-room, with none to care for us but Antoun. Zakhia's kind-hearted family had gathered round us weeping, and protecting us from the local priest, a sort of crack-brained fellow who wanted to insist on treating us. I have been assured that during the whole of this period my sister never gave one sign of consciousness.

Dr. Suquet, to whom the direction of the treatment to be followed was naturally confided, soon realised, alas! that she was beyond human help. Every effort to create reaction failed. She could not swallow the sulphate of quinine, large doses of which are the supreme remedy for these terrible attacks. Oh! can it be that if the new treatment had begun a few hours earlier it might have saved her? One agonising thought, at all events, will never leave me. If we had stayed at Beyrout, the attack would not have been escaped, indeed, but in all probability Dr. Suquet would have been called on in time to overcome it.

All that Monday my loving, noble-hearted sister lay fading away. On Tuesday, September 24th, at three o'clock in the morning, she died. The Maronite priest, who was sent for at the last moment, gave her extreme unction according to the rites of his Church. Many heartfelt tears were shed beside her corpse. But oh! my God, who would have thought my Henriette would have passed away within a couple of feet of where I was without my being able to receive her farewell sigh? Yes; but for the fatal swoon that seized me on the Sunday night, I do believe my kisses and the sound of my voice would have kept life in her for a few hours more, long enough, perhaps, to have saved her in the end. I cannot persuade myself her loss of consciousness was so utter that I could not have roused her. Once or twice, in feverish dreams, a terrible doubt has risen up before me. I have fancied I have heard her voice calling to me from the vault where she was laid! The presence of French doctors at her deathbed of course disposes of this horrible supposition. But the thought that she was waited on by strangers, that she was touched by menial hands, that I could not even follow her to the grave, and let my tears bear witness to the very earth how deeply I had loved her — that if her sight returned for even a moment's space before she left this world, my face was not before her — will weigh me down for ever, and poison all my future happiness. If she felt herself dying without knowing me at her side, if she realised that I was agonising close to her, and she not able to watch over me, oh! then that angelic creature must have passed away with a hell of anguish in her heart! Physical consciousness is so infinitely greater than its appearance or than our recollection of it, that I find it hard sometimes to feel perfectly easy in my mind about this matter.

My constitution, less exhausted than my sister's, was able to bear the tremendous dose of quinine which had been administered to me. Towards the Tuesday morning, about an hour before the time at which my beloved passed away, I began to recover my senses. A proof that I was much more conscious on the Sunday, and even during my delirium, than my memory of that time would indicate, lies in the fact that my first question was an inquiry after my sister's health. "She is very ill," they replied. I kept on repeating the same question through the half-slumber in which I lay. At last they answered — "She is dead!" It was no use trying to deceive me, for they were getting ready to carry me to Beyrout. I besought them to let me see her. They absolutely refused. They laid me in the very cot which was to have been used for her. I was completely stunned. The fearful misfortune that had befallen me hung over me like some hideous dream. I was devoured with agonising thirst. I thought I was with her, as in a burning vision, at Aphaca, where the Adonis river rises, under the huge walnut trees which grow above the waterfall. She was sitting by my side on the cool sward, I held a glass of icy water to her failing lips, and together we plunged into the life-giving spring, weeping, and borne down with over-mastering sadness. It was not till two days later that I recovered full consciousness, and that my disaster broke upon me in all its fearful reality.

Monsieur Gaillardot remained behind us at Amschit to superintend my poor sister's funeral. The villagers, who had grown much attached to her, followed her bier. There was no possibility of embalming the corpse; some temporary resting-place had to be found. For this purpose Zakhia offered the tomb of Mikhaël Tobia, standing at the end of the village, near a pretty chapel, and shaded by beautiful palm-trees. All he asked was that when the remains were removed, an inscription should commemorate the fact that a Frenchwoman's body had rested in the vault. She rests there still. I shrink from the idea of taking her from the beautiful mountains where she had been so happy, from the midst of the worthy folk she loved, to lay her in one of those dreary modern cemeteries she held in such deep horror. Some day, of course, she must come back to me, but who can tell what corner of the world shall hold my grave? Let her wait for me then under the palms of Amschit, in the land of the antique mysteries, by sacred Byblos!

We know not the exact relationship between great

souls and the principle of eternity. But if, as all things lead us to believe, conscious existence is but a passing communion with the universe, designed to carry us more or less close to the divine essence, surely into such souls as hers it is that immortality is breathed! If it be true that man possess the power of shaping a great moral personality after a divine model, not of his choosing, compact in equal parts of his own individuality and the ideal pattern, absolutely instinct with life, it must be so. Matter is not, because it has no separate existence. The atom does not live, because it has no consciousness of life.

The soul it is that lives when it has left a faithful mark on the eternal history of goodness and of truth. Was this destiny ever more perfectly accomplished than in my sister's person? She never could have developed a higher degree of perfection than that she had attained when she was taken from us in all the full maturity of her nature. She had reached the acme of the virtuous life. Her view of earthly things could never have been broader — the cup of her devotion and her love was full to overflowing.

Ah! what she ought to have had — there is no gainsaying it — is a happier life. I had dreamt of all sorts of trifling sweet delights — I had woven a thousand fancied pleasures for her. I pictured her in her old age, honoured like a parent, proud of me, resting at last in unalloyed repose. I had vowed her good and noble heart, so tender it was apt to bleed, should rest at last in calm — I had almost said in selfish peace. God only permitted her the steepest, hardest paths. She died well-nigh without reward. The harvest-hour, wherein men sit them down to rest and look back over the weariness and suffering of bygone days, never struck for her.

To say truth, she never gave reward a thought. That spirit of self-interest which so often mars the devotion inspired by positive religious beliefs, and provokes the idea that virtue is only practised for the sake of what it is likely to produce, had no place in her great soul. When her religious faith failed her, her faith in duty never flinched, because it was the echo of her innate nobility. Virtue was no result of theory in her case; it was the outcome of the unconscious bent of all her nature. She did good for the sake of doing good, and not to earn her ultimate salvation. She loved all goodness and beauty without any of that calculating spirit which seems to say to God, "If heaven and hell had no existence, I would not love Thee!"

But God will not permit His saints to see corruption. Oh, heart that ever nursed a flame of tenderest love! Oh, brain, the seat of thought so exquisitely pure! Oh, lovely eyes, shining with tender light! Oh, long and dainty hand, so often clasped in mine! — the thought that you are fallen away to dust thrills me with horror!

But sublunary things are all but types and shadows. The true eternal part of every living soul is that which binds it to eternity. Man's immortality is in God's memory. And there my Henriette, in everlasting radiance and eternal sinlessness, lives, with a life a thousand times more real than when she wrestled, in her feeble strength, to create her spiritual personality, and, cast upon a world which never knew how to understand her, strove obstinately to attain the perfect state.

Let us hold fast her memory as a precious demonstration of those eternal truths whereof every virtuous life contributes proof.

Personally I have never doubted the reality of the Moral Law. But now I see clearly that all the logic of the universal system must come to naught if such lives as hers were nothing but a delusion and a snare.

LETTERS OF
ERNEST AND HENRIETTE RENAN

1842–1845

I

MADEMOISELLE RENAN, *care of Comte André Zamoysky, Palfi Palace, Josefsplatz, Vienna, Austria.*

ISSY, *March* 23, 1842.

At last, dearest Henriette, I have your longed-for letter. For more than a month my mother and Alain have been assuring me I should get it shortly. Day by day I have been on the tiptoe of expectation, watching every post, and never dreaming such an unlucky incident had retarded my happiness. This expectation, long drawn out, is responsible for my long delay in writing you, for I did not want to do that till I had your letter. I have it at last, dear Henriette, and I'm happy! I hasten to reply, and one of the long afternoons we have here shall be spent in talking with you. How long it is since I have had that pleasure!

More separation, my dear sister! Vienna was not far enough away! The whole of Europe must lie betwixt us, it seems! I do trust this is the end, and that you will not go beyond Poland, at all events.

Nothing smaller in area than Russia could suffice, indeed, to calm my fears and set a limit to your wanderings. Dismay fills my imagination when it dwells on the immense space that parts us. If any one had told us, when we were living in the depths of Brittany, that a very few years would see you buried in the wilds of Poland, we should have held him a wild dreamer. Yet he would have told us truly. A strange thing, life! I cannot describe all the thoughts I think, especially when I go back to the earliest period my memory reaches, to the time when we hid our poverty at Lannion, to the not less unhappy days of our struggles at Tréguier, when we shuddered at the very idea of a separation of a hundred and twenty leagues. And now behold us parted, not by a province or two even, but by kingdoms and by peoples. Such is human life! And should it all end in happiness (which, in our case, means reunion), we shall be fortunate indeed. If this does not come to pass, 'twill not be by any fault of yours, my dear good Henriette. And I have the sweetest, steadiest hope of it. Well, I know you will never endure to lead an idle, nerveless, springless life. Ah! no; I know you far too well to think that could ever be your taste, nor, for the matter of that, mine either. That is not what I mean. But I do believe all else in life would be tame and empty and hollow without that charm we find in friendship, and that never is so solid and steadfast as between those who are bound by ties of blood. This, then, dear Henriette, is the end I love to fancy to all our labours. The future again! How incorrigible is human nature! We never think of the present — we are always longing for some coming joy! Well, after all, we are not far wrong. This present of ours is so sad and wretched, we do well to lighten the burden, at all events, by some glimpse of a future we always fancy brightly coloured. Ah! how right Pascal was when he said, "Nous ne vivons pas, mais nous espérons de vivre!" Hope is our life, indeed — our only life.

I have barely escaped falling into a philosophical disquisition, which might have been better placed. But I like talking over all my occupations with you, and at this moment philosophy is my study — indeed, I may say, my favourite one. Thanks to the prejudice accumulated during a course of rhetoric, I expected, when I began philosophy, to find it a tiresome and difficult study, bristling with abstract propositions, and as barbarous in doctrine as it often is in expression. But I soon got rid of this mistaken idea, and, far from regretting the exchange, I would not go back now to the declamations of rhetoric for anything on earth. It represents the science of words as opposed to that of things. Imagination, which in rhetoric is all in all, does indeed serve but little in philosophy, where reason reigns supreme. But surely the man who prefers the pleasures of the imagination to those of reason is no judge of true intellectual enjoyment. Yet we must not expect philosophy to offer the absolute certainties which distinguish mathematics, for instance. The number of systems of philosophy in existence prove this: where certainty is, variety of system is non-existent. Some portions of philosophy are as inflexible indeed, and as severely reasoned out, as a mathematical problem. Yet even here the domain of hypothesis is rarely quitted. But these same hypotheses are deeply interesting, and frequently seem to touch truth as nearly as our weak reason is permitted to approach it. The proper function of philosophy, indeed, is not so much to give very definite notions as to scatter a cloud of prejudices. It is astonishing, once one applies one's mind to it, to realise that you have hitherto been the sport of half a hundred erroneous ideas, rooted in general opinion, custom, or education. This gives the deathblow to one's ideal conception of the beauty of things. They appear as they really are, and one is very much astounded to find matters one believed decided once for all ranked as unsettled problems. Realising these numberless mistakes, one's first inclination is to universal doubt. But that is false reasoning again, and the German philosophers, who are by no means over-inclined to certainty, do not go so far. Kant, even, the father of modern sceptics, holds back on that head. It is this craving for *truth*, which philosophy engenders, that makes mathematical study so fascinating. There, at least, truth is to be found, absolute, *indispensable*. And this study is the essential complement of a course of philosophy. All my own taste for it, which three years of literary study had not utterly quenched, has now revived. All I have had to do is, so to speak, to stir the embers. This year we are on pure mathematics; next year we shall apply them in mechanics, physical science, and so forth. As to my German, I am the merest beginner, and, in spite of all you say, it will be long, I doubt, before you find anything of a rival in me. Up till now, I have rarely been able to give any considerable time to it. As soon as I began to study philosophy, I perceived I should do no more than wisely if I gave my undivided attention to so all-important a subject. Now I have mastered the key of that position, I shall be able to apply myself to it still more fully. We really have great facilities here for learning living languages; for the varied nationalities of those amongst whom we live give us opportunities of talking with them in their mother-tongues and forming our pronunciation — always the most difficult thing to acquire in a modern language — on that of natives.

Having thus lengthily explained the object of my studies, dearest Henriette, I must say a word concerning my new abiding-place, of which your recollection of St. Nicolas can give you no idea. The two houses are radically different. While St. Nicolas, as a residence, was cramped, confined, and dreary, Issy is spacious, pleasant, and cheerful. While at St. Nicolas the differences between master and pupil were strongly marked, here they are imperceptible. Study here is as serious as it was flimsy there. But there are certain advantages on the other side. That personal care of each pupil which was so scrupulous at St. Nicolas is quite neglected here. Each one has to do for himself, both at his work and for his material wants. And so it should be, as it seems to me, for these pupils are not children, as we were at St. Nicolas. There is no special mark here whereby masters and principals are distinguished from students. Equality reigns, not amongst these latter only, but between them and their instructors. This makes life freer, less constrained. As to the pupils themselves, they are more numerous, and more serious too as to their work, than at St. Nicolas. And some of them have remarkable talent to boot. This indeed is a strong point at St. Sulpice. As it is a seminary for the whole of France, and not for Paris only, each bishop sends his strongest men, to secure the best teaching for them. Thus the cleverness of the majority is above the average, and narrow-mindedness is quite the exception — a wonderful thing in any seminary.

Your dear visits are the one thing lacking in my life. It is a great trial to me, I confess, not to have one soul to whom I can say a word about my loved ones. And your letters are my greatest happiness. Has Alain mentioned his plan of living with our dear mother to you? He dropped a word about it when I saw him at the end of the holidays; since then I have heard nothing of it. I should be very glad, for my part, if it were carried out, for our poor mother really leads a sad and lonely life.

Thank you, dear Henriette, for your loving care of me. Your bank-note will come in very opportunely, for though our dear mother sent me a remittance not long ago, it was exhausted very soon, as I had to get a new cassock, &c. Yours will enable me to supply my German library, the scantiness of which partly paralyses my progress in that tongue. I shall owe you everything, poor Henriette! You have been a second mother to me, and all my heart is given to you and my mother and Alain. Often have I reflected what a blessing it is for us all, who are fated to be so far apart, that we love each other so fondly. The pain of separation is diminished a thousand-fold by our affection. Do endeavour to reconcile our mother to the idea of your leaving Vienna, when you write to her. Try to make the distance seem less. I saw, during my holidays, how the thought of all your journeys affected her. We must spare her all the anxiety we can. She really needs repose after the many storms of her past life.

Farewell, dear Henriette! My thoughts of you are my dearest joy. My pleasure in your letter is dashed by the feeling that many months may roll by before another reaches me. Now you know my address, pray give me that happiness a little oftener — directly, indirectly, I care not how, so long as I have your letters! Farewell once more! You know how much I love you. Always, dearest, best of sisters, will you be my joy and happiness. — Your beloved brother,

E. RENAN.

N.B. — You can write me quite freely. Our letters are never opened, and we get them as soon as they arrive.

II

MDLLE. RENAN, *care of M. le Comte André Zamoysky, Zwierziniec, Poland,*[1] via *Cracow and Zawichost.*

ISSY, *September* 15, 1842.

The distance between us is so heartbreaking, that I dare not complain of the rarity of your letters, my dear Henriette. Yet it tries me to have nothing but indirect tidings of you, through my mother and Alain.[2] They suffice indeed to subdue the anxiety I might otherwise feel, but they cannot satisfy that yearning for direct intercourse with you which has become a part of my being.

I long for volumes, and I have scarcely had a word. If we were less devoted at heart, we should be almost strangers to each other. But that, my dearest Henriette, is a danger we need never fear.

You probably know I am not going to spend my holidays in Brittany this year. The fact of not seeing my mother and the friends I am so sincerely attached to has caused me some regret indeed, but that must give way to the real advantages of putting off my

---

[1] As the reader will have gathered from the perusal of "My Sister Henriette," Mdlle. Renan occupied a post as governess in Poland. Her correspondence with her brother was subject to protracted delays.

[2] Ernest Renan's elder brother.

journey till next season. For as our finances do not permit of our making it annual, I would much rather delay it for another twelvemonth. I shall then have brought both my course of philosophy and my residence at Issy to a close, and the trip into Brittany will be a very pleasant change before I enter the seminary in Paris. Besides, this last year has flown so quickly that I feel as if I had only just got back; my impressions of Brittany have never seemed fresher. And then, my kind Henriette, how should I make any complaint when I think of you, and the courage with which you bear your exile, far longer and more trying than my own, which is none at all, indeed, except in so far as that I am parted from the objects of my affection. To wind up, Issy is a spot where a man may spend a very pleasant holiday. The situation is charming, the park is perfectly delightful. It offers a quiet and repose most admirably suited to my tastes. I can work and think in peace. There is good society in the place — some very pleasant company indeed — and one is free as air. In fact, I am so comfortable here, I find it hard to move, and during this past year I have sometimes been three or four months without leaving the house. The walks are all so long, and so uninteresting to me since your departure, that my courage fails me each time I ought to go out of doors, and I only pay the most indispensable of visits.

We have just ended our first yearly course of philosophy and mathematics. It is curious what a revelation these grave studies are to a mind just escaped from the comparative frivolities of a course of rhetoric. One makes more progress in a year than the human race does in the space of a century. Things strike one in such a different way. So many errors and prejudices appear where one had looked to find nothing but truth, that one is half tempted to embrace a universal scepticism. That is the first impression caused by a study of philosophy. The uncertainty of human knowledge, and the instability of all opinions founded on human reasoning alone, strike one deeply. If nature allowed it, and if it were not as absurd to reject all truth as to embrace all error, one would be inclined to universal doubt. This is but a negative result indeed, and we should have to moderate our praise of philosophy were its sole effect to be the weakening of every conviction. But it has others, infinitely precious, especially when studied in connection with mathematics and physics, from which it never should be parted. Thus taken, it creates a power of closest reasoning, it makes us look at all things in simplicity and truth (a thing as rare as it is difficult); and above all, it teaches us not to live blind amongst the marvels that surround us, more even in the intellectual than in the physical order of things, and which too generally pass unnoticed. This again — the power of appreciating the wonderful, wherever apparent — is one of the most striking results of the study of philosophy. If it does not solve every problem, at all events it teaches us to recognise their existence. I like the methods of your German thinkers, in spite of their being somewhat sceptical and pantheistic. If ever you go to Königsberg, I pray you make a pilgrimage in my name to the tomb of Kant.

This taste of mine for meditation, joined to the perfect peace and intellectual freedom I enjoy in this retreat, where no special form of occupation is imposed on me, has enabled me to think a little about myself and my own future. I must admit I had not given the subject much consideration previously, content to follow whatever outside impulse was impressed on me. I have begun at last to examine it attentively. The first thing to strike me was the huge influence the earliest actions of life have on one's future, coupled with the thoughtlessness with which they are performed. Then all you have so often told me, but which I never understood before, came back to me. My first fear was lest I might have done something foolhardy already, and then I rejoiced at having as yet taken no decisive or irrevocable step. But after ripe reflection, after having studied my own tastes and nature thoroughly, after having closely considered the character of the profession I propose to enter, with the various careers it opens up to me, and the probable characteristics of my future colleagues, having again carefully weighed my own convictions (which might well be somewhat shaken by my first attempt at philosophical study, so apt to heat the brain), I have come to believe I have no reason so far to regret the action I have taken, and if I had the power to choose afresh, I would repeat it.

I will not say I have not discovered enormous drawbacks on every point I have referred to; I will even acknowledge to the sister from whom I have no secrets that I can never accept many ideas which general opinion classes as peculiarly pertaining to the state in question; that if I were to be doomed to live with certain of my colleagues, whose frivolity, duplicity, and crawling toadyism is well known to me, I would far rather choose to spend my days cut off from all mankind. And I have realised that I shall be submitting myself to an authority which is apt to be suspicious, yet to which I will never bend, if in so doing I commit an act of meanness. But I perceived these same enormous drawbacks elsewhere, allied moreover to a thousand others more worthy of the name of downright impracticability than of mere disadvantage, and no other condition of life, it seemed to me, would give me greater facilities for following my natural bent. My great end and object, this many a day, has been a life of retirement, freedom, and independence, not devoid of usefulness — a life, in other words, of laborious study. I believe I have made certain of the fact that I am quite unfitted for what is vulgarly called the world, that is to say, for life in clubs and drawing-rooms. All the qualities I have not are indispensable for that, and none of those I have would serve me in it. I have no taste for it besides; I was not born for trifling and for foolery, and the world, if so it calls itself, seems to me full of them.

It is not the fervour of religious zeal which makes me say this. Oh no, indeed! I have no weakness in that direction either. Philosophy has a wonderful power of moderating such excesses, and the only result to be dreaded from its study is too violent a reaction. I hated such extremes in former days on purely religious grounds. I hate them now in the light of reason and philosophy, and also, I confess, by my own instinct. A life devoid of thought and meditation, without a moment given to self-examination, is utterly incompatible with the deepest needs of my soul. This granted, I must look on any career which does not admit of study and quiet thought as closed to me. This simplifies the whole question and makes selection easy. Moreover, the sublimity of the sacerdotal functions, when looked on from the highest and truest point of view, has always struck me. Even if Christianity were but a dream, the priesthood would always be a type of the divine. I know, indeed, that, great as it is in itself, it has been belittled by its human representatives. They must needs drag it down to their own level. I can even understand, even while holding it as mere prejudice, the scorn with which some people view it. But that contempt only concerns themselves, and it is evident that a priesthood which is by necessity numerically strong is bound to number a certain proportion of mean and vile natures in its ranks. These must degrade it in the sight of those who, in their superficial view of life, instead of looking at the matter in its truest light, see only the man where they ought to see his ministry. Besides, as aforesaid, that is only their opinion, and I believe myself, by God's mercy, to be above opinion.

I have now given you the result of my ponderings on this important question with that complete frankness which you have always found in me. Not that I have ceased thinking about it. I am still trying, on the contrary, to clear and settle all my ideas on the subject; but this is the most positive conclusion I have as yet arrived at.

I will beg you not to mention my doubts to our mother. If they should have no other outcome than to confirm me in my past intentions, she had better remain in ignorance of them. They would make her anxious. But never think she has influenced my decision on this head. No one could desire more perfect freedom than that she has left me in.

I had a letter from that dear mother of ours the day before yesterday. She seems well and cheerful. The day before that I had one from Alain, equally satisfactory, though complaining of the avalanche of work which leaves him without a moment to himself. When will that poor fellow enjoy a little peace and quietness? I hope soon to hear from you. I am rather afraid this letter may not reach you. I always pay the postage as far as Huninguen. Perhaps I ought to send the letters by another frontier? Tell me in your next.

Farewell, my dear good Henriette. If the whole universe lay between us, I could not love you more, nor think of you more constantly. I do not try to express my affection; you know it better than I can tell it you. — Your brother and your friend,

E. RENAN.

III

October 30, 1842.

It is about twelve days since your letter of 15th September reached me, my beloved Ernest. May the joy these lines of mine give you, equal that yours caused me! Yes, dearest one; a continent lies betwixt us, and judging by the sparseness of our letters, a careless onlooker might think that in our case, too, separation had induced indifference. We in our hearts feel such a disaster cannot reach us, for you can never doubt my passionate tenderness and my boundless devotion, wherever I may be. My poor boy! I live on my memories. But the thought of those I love is ever with me. What could turn me from it? . . .

Ever since I received your letter, my Ernest, I have been pondering it deeply. I cannot help shuddering as I read of the questions which agitate your mind, and realise that you are absorbed by these solemn thoughts at an age when life is generally so frivolous and careless. Yet, in spite of my tender love for you, I cannot but rejoice to see you take such a serious view of matters which so many others judge lightly, or in accordance with the passions of their own hearts. Yes, my dear friend, those first steps in life do often have an irreparable influence on all its future, as I deeply felt when I used so constantly to appeal to your consideration of that truth. People take the fancies of a boy of fourteen for serious tastes, without considering that a youth of sixteen and a man of thirty are two well-nigh totally different beings.

My darling Ernest, I cannot say it too often — I ask it with well-nigh maternal fondness — do not bind yourself by any hasty action. Wait till you can thoroughly understand them before you accept engagements which must determine your whole existence. I might, perhaps, my dear, lay stress on the influence over you which my affection and the experience of my much-tried life should give me, but I will refrain, because I have faith in your own reason, and I will always be content to appeal to that. You say truly, my Ernest, you were not born to lead a careless life, and I should agree with you that the one you dream of would be the best, according to your tastes, if it were capable of realisation. Better than any other woman, perhaps, this sister of yours can comprehend the charm of a life of retirement, free and independent, laborious, and, above all things, useful. But where are you to find it? Such independence, I believe, if not impossible, is at all events granted to very few in any state of life. In my own person I have never known it. How then can I dare to hope it will be your portion in a society based on the hierarchical principle, and ruled, as you rightly discern, by an authority which is apt to be suspicious?

We must not deceive ourselves. Authority of a kind exists in every career. But surely in this particular one it is to be specially dreaded, since you are bound under it by an irrevocable oath.

I only suggest this to you as a question, leaving you entire liberty of action and power of decision. To it I will add another proceeding from it. Is an ecclesiastic a free agent? Is he not forced to follow the direction of his superiors? I will not contest what you say about the dignity of the office. Truly, if all who entered it took your view, nothing could be greater, more worthy of a noble nature, than to devote one's life to softening sorrow, to preaching and practising the sublime truths of the Gospel. I will only add this one word to your own reflections. You suffer now, my Ernest, because you see personal interest and ambition where your pure and upright soul had dreamt of finding nothing but self-sacrifice and devotion; you have realised that many of those who seem vowed to their great mission are very far from understanding it, or being worthy of it in practice. But will you be suffered to choose the way you would desire to follow? Is there not a certain indicated path from which you will not be allowed to swerve? Are not custom and the majority stronger than the minority and duty?

Once more I say it, dear brother, I only suggest these questions to you; may your reason and your conscience help you to solve them. I have had much experience in life; I love you with all the strength of a devoted heart, and yet I shrink from giving any direct advice in this particular. If it had rested with me to guide your choice of a career, I should not have been content to leave you perfectly free while you were still a mere child. I should have thought it right to hold out for a long time before yielding to your inclination. I take a different line now, because I believe you to be sensible beyond your years, and because I feel your decision must be yours alone, uninfluenced by any other opinion. But that is an additional motive for my entreating you not to judge hastily in a matter of so great importance. Wait till you have reached man's estate, and are in a position to gauge what you reject and what you accept. Even should you persist in your present opinions, some experience of life will, anyhow, be necessary to you before you undertake to lead others through it. How can a young man of four or five and twenty, who has never quitted his scholastic seclusion, be capable of guiding and supporting people who are constantly involved in struggles of every kind?

Let no consideration of family feeling stand in your way. I beseech you, as a personal favour, not to risk the whole of your life's happiness to soothe the qualms of your own kind heart. Has not the consolation of all my labour been the thought that it might serve my dear one — the child of my adoption — my beloved Ernest? One day, if I am spared, your turn will come, if indeed there can ever be any question of repaying a debt to one we love.

Make yourself perfectly easy as to my secrecy as regards our mother. I feel how vitally important that is. You know that, short of actual dissimulation, I am inclined to keep her in ignorance of anything likely to make her uneasy. Her peace of mind is the chief object of my life. Tell me your whole thought always, and be sure it will never go beyond me. Write to me oftener, I entreat you. I need to read your heart to feel once more, and always, that I am your closest friend. Sometimes, doubtless, as to-day, my answers may repeat things I have already told you over and over again, but that will be because they so preoccupy my thoughts. My dearest child, remember, whatever befalls you, you have a sister to share your every feeling, whose dearest and closest attachment is to you. Take anything I say as being devoid of every personal feeling, and solely dictated by the tenderest interest in you, and the deepest desire to see you happy. Happy! . . . can that be, in this troubled and sorrowful world? And, without reckoning the blows of fate and of our fellow-men, is not one's own heart a bottomless spring of restlessness and misery?

What you tell me of your liking for the German philosophers pleases but does not surprise me. Germany is the classic home of quiet reverie and metaphysical argument. The other European nations will find it hard to bring their schools of philosophy to the level reached by the German thinkers. The contemplative turn of the Teutonic mind, the quiet habits of the national life, the very climate, all tend to develop that leisurely mode of thought which is part of the North German character, and one of the greatest enjoyments known to its possessors. The French mind, quick as it is, and fascinating, and prompt at grasping an idea, is too volatile, generally speaking, to be profoundly philosophic. The Englishman is cold and calculating, submitting everything to the chilliest argument. But the German, who carries his native simplicity and good-nature everywhere, even into the most elevated questions, allows himself to feel and think and grow poetic over everything. If you prosecute your studies in the tongue of Kant and Hegel, of Goethe and Schiller, you will discover many delightful charms in its rich and varied literature. I can only lay hold on driblets of its wealth, but even that little has often given me great pleasure. Unluckily, instead of making progress, I have lost ground since coming to Poland. We live in a desert, where masters are not to be had, and working alone, I find myself checked at every step. Study, dear Ernest, helps one to forget many a vexation. By its means one lives in a world of fancy, which, whatever it be, is always superior to the reality. The less I am able to enjoy it, the more I appreciate its quiet delights.

I spent the month of August and part of September at Warsaw, about sixty leagues from this place. We have only been back about a month. The only way to form an idea of the country I inhabit is to fancy huge monotonous sandy plains, which would make you think yourself in Arabia or in Africa, but for the endless forests of birch and pine which break them up, and recall one's close proximity to northern latitudes. And indeed the climate does not permit you to forget it. It has been cold already, as cold as it would be in Paris in late December. I saw snow falling as I passed through Galicia on the 30th of April, and on the 14th of October, again, walking on the river-bank at midday, I found icicles. Spring, summer, and autumn are here crowded into a space of five months. All the rest is winter.

We are to spend the one we are just entering upon in this solitude, of which nothing in France can give the slightest conception. The house is a very fine one, surrounded by huge forests, and here we live, cut off from the whole world. I should be indifferent to that if all correspondence were not so slow and difficult. It is not the want of local news that I regret, but news of my beloved and distant home. Some of my letters come fairly quickly, but others are delayed, arrive open. . . .

You see, dear Ernest, that my love of work and sedentary tastes are a blessing to me here. What could I find outside them? The Polish peasant is the most poverty-stricken, brutish creature you can conceive of. Two-thirds of the town population are Jews, filthy and loathsome creatures, living in a state of abjectness which exceeds all imagination. Nowhere is the spirit of fanaticism and religious hatred carried further than in this country, nowhere are the passions of men more often cloaked under the name of godliness. Jew-beating is a good deed in a Christian. To rob the Christian is the sole aim and object of the Jew. Nor is this all. The Christian sects are not one whit more tolerant of each other, and on every hand you see men hating each other in the name of Him whose teaching was all charity and peace. "Father, forgive them: they know not what they do."

I had a letter yesterday from our mother, dated

22nd September. She seems well and easy in her mind. I sent her a sum of money from Warsaw, out of which I asked her to send you a hundred and fifty francs to begin your winter with. But I begged her not to stint herself, and if she has not sent you the money I will arrange to let you have it otherwise. Tell me frankly whether she has or not, and do not mention it to any one else. Be quite easy, my dear child; I can manage it all. I have very few personal expenses. Though I have to live in a world which you justly call vain and frivolous, I take my simple tastes there with me. I cannot think I acquire greater merit by wearing a smarter gown. Farewell, my dear Ernest! I find it hard to end my letter. I have cramped my writing, and filled up all the corners of my paper, so as to have more space to write on. Remember me and love me, and never doubt my unchangeable affection.

Farewell! in deepest tenderness, again farewell!

IV

Mdlle. Renan, *care of M. le Comte André Zamoysky, Zwierziniec, Zawichost,* via *Cracow, Poland.*

Issy, *January* 17, 1843.

I have been talking to you, as it were, my dearest Henriette, ever since your last letter reached me. The boundless affection it breathes is very precious to my soul, and the wise and true considerations you suggest are the constant subject of my thoughts. I cannot tell you all the contrary feelings and conflicting desires its repeated perusal has aroused within me. I had long since begun to look seriously at things I had scarcely glanced at, had even shrunk from closely examining previously. Your letter has plunged me yet deeper into solemn thought. The picture you draw of the innumerable difficulties to which my choice of the priesthood would expose me is no more than what my own imagination had traced. A distrustful and often bigoted authority, an indissoluble vow, the obligation (if indeed it is one) to follow beaten tracks even if they be tortuous, the frequent necessity of calling those whom one is driven to despise by the name of brother and colleague — all this had occurred to me, magnified even by the shock to my imagination of discovering obstacles where I had anticipated none. The singular agreement of your ideas with the impression which had taken hold of me has struck me deeply, and makes me fear it is only too correct. I have often wished some decisive blow might fall from one side or the other to end my painful doubts. And oftener still I have rejoiced to think my liberty — the most precious thing we have, and for that very reason the hardest to preserve — is still my own.

In considering the great question which fills all my gravest thoughts, I always lay it down as a principle that every man desirous of knowing to what estate he is called must seek the solution of that problem, the most important and the most neglected in existence, in the study of his own nature. Its true indications are to be found in the bent and inclinations of each individual, and I believe the reason so few men fall into their proper place is that there are so few who know themselves thoroughly. Well, one point alone, I repeat, has been made clear by my inquiry — an enduring and exclusive taste for a life of quiet and retirement, of study and reflection. All the ordinary occupations of mankind are dull and insipid to me, their pleasures would be my boredom, the motives which govern them in their different states of life simply disgust me. Hence I conclude without hesitation that I am fit for none of them. Even the teaching profession, though better suited to my sedentary and studious tastes, is repugnant to me, on account of the manœuvres necessary to getting above the dust of elementary instruction. But, you will say, does the ecclesiastical state offer you greater facilities for following your favourite bent? Alas! my dear Henriette, I say it again, I do not mince the matter; my view of things has been and is too close a one for me to have any illusion. That would be unpardonable henceforward, for it would manifestly arise from my own thoughtlessness. But what else can I do? Any career full of exterior occupations runs counter to my tastes. There is no time for self-communion, for reflection; one is a perfect stranger to one's own self. A completely private life, if I may so express it, would be my delight; but that it seems to me stained with selfishness, I should indeed live *to* myself, but also *for* myself alone. And besides, could I endure the thought of being dependent on those I love? But the priesthood unites every advantage of such a life without any of its drawbacks. The priest is the guardian of wisdom and counsel, he is a man of study and of meditation, and with it all he is the servant of his brethren.

This happy mixture of publicity and privacy, of

solitude for one's own sake and sacrifice for that of others, would be my beau ideal of a happy and completely rounded life. Why should it be disturbed by human fault? though that indeed must be expected. All that is fairest and purest changes and undergoes corruption in its passage through the hands of men. What is greater and more beneficent than religion? and what more baleful and more mean as practised by the human race, which uses it as the instrument of its passions, and drags it down to their mean level? What can be more sublime than the sacerdotal office? yet what more vile when looked at in the person of those who exercise its functions in a shameful spirit of self-interest? But he who seeks the highest and noblest truth must acquire the habit of raising himself above the superficial view, must put aside all contemplation of individual men, and look into the heart of things.

The men around me (I speak of the principals of this house) would indeed be very likely to prepossess me favourably, did I not remind myself how few there are like them. The seminaries of St. Sulpice and of Issy are under a congregation of priests independent of episcopal authority, and who have always been remarkable for the moderation of their views. M. Cousin has just published a book in which he gives them well-deserved praise. The resemblance

I notice between my own aspirations and those of our Superior has given me great confidence in him. I have even gone so far as to touch on the subject now engaging our attention, under the reserve, of course, which can never be dropped outside one's own family. I have told him frankly, "Sir, I confess I should be glad not to have to give any one an account of my actions. A life of freedom and independence is what would suit me best." "Alack! dear friend," he answered, "where are you to find it?" He seemed to say, "I too have sought it, and I have sought in vain." I recognise the fact that, in a century like ours, he only who commands is free. That thought alone should suffice to inspire me with ambition. And then there is a reflection which often occurs to me, and which consoles me. Every man has one certain refuge, to withdraw into himself, and in the enjoyment of his own internal resources to indemnify himself for his exterior servitude. The Author of our being conferred an inestimable benefit on us in that internal liberty of ours, safe from all external constraint, in the case at least of those who know how to preserve it. For how very few, again, enjoy this blessing! If I were making this inquiry coldly and without any instinctive bias, it would not cause me so much pain. But it is an unspeakable grief to me to think how much of my poor mother's happiness depends on it. This will not influence me, for my conscience forbids it; but I have to gather all my strength together to prevent it. For I assure you from the bottom of my heart, I would willingly be unhappy all my life sooner than give her one hour of sorrow.

Go on talking to me, dearest Henriette, in fullest frankness. Tell me your whole thought, and fear no indiscretion. You can send your letters direct to me; they are never opened. And besides, we are allowed to go and fetch them from the porter at post-time. I send you this one through Alain. The prepayment of the postage to the frontier is too complicated a business for the mind of the servant to whom I have to confide it. I have the greatest trouble in making him take it in, and still greater fear that he will fail in carrying it out.

The routine studies of philosophy and physics which occupy me this year still have their old attraction, and are a real support to me. All you say in your letter about the charm of study is delightfully true, and I verify it every day. Our professor of physics is a man of first-class merit. His digressions on the history of science and its true spirit are deeply interesting. As to our professor of philosophy, he is a novice, but day by day I grow more convinced that the mediocrity of its professor is no drawback in that department of study. To learn philosophy well, you must practically do your own reasoning. I am now reading, with extreme enjoyment, the philosophical works of Malebranche, undoubtedly the finest thinker and the most merciless logician that ever existed. I find a double satisfaction in them. Malebranche certainly was a bold thinker, and yet he was a priest, nay, more, a member of a religious congregation, and he lived in peace at an epoch when the secular arm and the spirit of the age united to give ecclesiastical authority even greater pride and power than it now possesses. So man's own weight inclines him on the side of hope.

Space fails me, dear kind sister, and I tremble at the thought that even within a month this letter may not have reached you, and that several may elapse before I can receive an answer.

I entreat you to let me hear as soon as possible. Farewell, beloved Henriette; my chief happiness is in my trust in you. Your affection is my greatest joy; try to imagine, then, how passionately I return it.

E. RENAN.

V

March 12, 1843.

My Ernest, — Your last letter broke upon my solitude about a fortnight ago. As no doubt of my tender affection can, I hope, enter your heart, I will not repeat that the reception of any proof of your regard is one of the liveliest joys that can be granted me. Yes! the thought of possessing one steady affection, amidst a life so full of instability and uncertainty, is sweet indeed.

Well, brother mine, on that happiness, at all events, the only one I have to give you, you may always reckon confidence in my tried and faithful love. Think sometimes of that deep devotion which so often gives me strength, and of which I would fain convince you utterly. Would I could share more directly all that which finds so sure an echo in my thought, that which is ever in my heart! Poor boy! How bitterly, as I read your letter, did I feel the hardship of our separation, now that both heart and soul in you are crying out for sympathy and support.

Let me come back, my well-beloved, to the ideas your letter to me expresses. You are perfectly right to say the taste and inclination of each man are the proper basis of any decision as to his ultimate fate. This is an evident truth, from which every one must deduce the same natural conclusion — that what would be happiness to some must often be a source of misery to others. When I constantly repeat that your resolution must be solely yours, I apply this principle to what is dearest to me on all this earth — to your peace, to your whole future, my poor child. Yet be sure of this, anxious as I am that your decision should be absolutely free, I am just as resolved to tell you my opinions and my fears without exception. I have never thought of forcing them upon you; I never shall. I desire merely to call your attention to the points which strike me, leaving you the most perfect liberty of action as regards taking my advice. Let this, I beg, be clearly understood between us. Yes, beloved friend, a life of solitude, of devotion to others, of complete independence, would certainly be the dream of every generous heart. Unhappily there is no such life on earth. Independence itself, that foremost of all good things, is but a brilliant figment of the fancy, and the Superior who has gained your confidence was very right to tell you, "Alas! where will you find it?" How often have I, like yourself, longed for it above all things? How often, in a splendid room, or before some sumptuous table, I have cried out in my heart, "O God! give me a crust of bread, and peace and freedom." Vain longings, which many another has nursed as hopelessly, which so very few are destined to attain. I agree with you that we are happy to possess some faculties which no man can coerce, and in the enjoyment of which we forget many an injustice; but believe me, my Ernest, I can assure you out of my own experience that it is only after many a struggle that our internal liberty can be secured from all external interference, and it is very hard to convince *our paymasters* that there are certain points whereon one owes no account save to God and one's own conscience.

These are painful truths to tell, more painful still to realise. But so things *are*, and so we must have courage to face them. Yet, granted that the conditions of human life must always tend towards slavery, there always remains the question of degree. Speaking as a woman and a governess, I have never known any but the minimum of independence; but, my dear Ernest, I am far from being convinced that the maximum of that priceless blessing is to be found in the career you think of embracing. In it especially the state of subordination alarms me for you, because there is no means of ever escaping it. I know, my dear, that my fears are open to many objections; if I did not, my language would be still more explicit.

I know, too, that I may be accused of giving judgment on a subject I have had no opportunity of examining closely, but you yourself admit that many of your hopes have melted away before your eyes. How then can I do otherwise than dread some fresh disappointment for you? Ernest! dearest friend! forgive me if I add my anxiety to your own, without saying a word to solve all your difficulties. Often do I accuse myself of deepening the abyss by thus leading you to probe your own thoughts, by searching them with you. But I cannot hide my slightest impression from you. How then could I conceal those which are foremost in my mind? You very truly remark, dear Ernest, that the manœuvres which ensure success in so many careers, even that of a teacher, are repugnant to your feelings. I will add that they might often offend your innate sense of uprightness. Public tuition, above a certain level, is a noble and attractive profession, inasmuch as it permits of a life of study and offers opportunities of usefulness to others. But it is difficult to reach that level, and the work at any lower one is very discouraging. You have had opportunities of judging this matter as closely as myself. Observe, however, that though I mention the great difficulties to be overcome before rising to professorial rank, I am far from believing it to be impossible. Others have done it, which proves its feasibility. And besides, it should be remembered that there is no profession in which the first steps are not difficult. Private tuition, in a man's case, is a career offering no outlook, which frequently renders any attempt at providing for the future utterly hopeless, and thus exposes him to a very pitiable old age. It is a life, too, in which dependence and subjection are strained to their uttermost limit, in which personal tastes must be perpetually sacrificed, and one's dearest studies put aside to overlook or assist pupils whose education bristles with difficulties caused by their own parents' follies. It is less fatiguing and laborious than public teaching, and yet, for a *man*, I should think this latter much to be preferred.

I do not attempt, my poor dear friend, to paint things gayer than they are. Always, alas! I must premise that life means suffering and struggle, and that it is a hard thing to make a position for oneself. Yet you must not lose courage. Far from it. If the path be rough, we have plenty of strength to carry us over its difficulties. In an upright spirit, a worthy end, a firm and unchanging will, we already possess the chief groundwork on which the edifice must rest. Whatever happens, my dear good brother, you will always have my active and zealous co-operation. My power to help is very small, unhappily, but that little, at all events, shall never fail you. Courage, then! go on in truth and wisdom and prudence, and be your choice what it may, at all events you will always be an honest man! Never let your confidence in me waver, be sure I shall always hold it sacred and most dear. I shall reckon on it all my life, just as I do on your returning the boundless affection I bear you. There is something so sweet in feeling such an inward strength, and in being able to lean on it without a taint of fear!

I have had no news of our dear good mother for a long time. Though this does not make me particularly anxious, it saddens me deeply, and that because I seem to have been neglectful of her in what has really been a very involuntary manner. Some three months ago I promised her a remittance which I had taken steps to send her. Living as I do in a country where I hardly know a soul, and where I consequently can do nothing by myself, I was obliged to apply, as always in such a case, to my pupil's father. He began by delaying, as rich people so often do, without meaning any harm, in money matters; then he went away from home, and has not yet returned. Our poor mother may be blaming me, while I have really neglected no means open to me of fulfilling my promise. I am always thinking she may be in difficulties, and that you too

... Oh Heavens! the thought afflicts me! Why cannot the rich consider that those who have no fortune but what they earn need to be regularly paid? Because, my dear, sad as it is to say it, man only enters into those sufferings he has himself endured — none others exist for him. How often I have had occasion to recognise this truth! I accuse no one. I excuse them rather. I hope soon to be able to rid me of this load which weighs so heavily on me.

Let me know when your vacation begins. I do not forget that you are to spend it with our dear mother this year, and I want to make my arrangements in advance for carrying out this delightful project. Write me, I beg of you, whenever that is possible. Ah! if you knew how happy it makes me to get a letter from you! Poor Ernest! how my heart ached when I left you! Farewell, my dear loved brother. Love me always, and be very sure that my fond memory turns to you in those moments when my heart seems weighed down with the sadness that so often haunts one in a foreign country, in spite of all one's efforts to be cheerful. Do not let this sadden you, dear Ernest. Though my life has been full of struggle, I have always been full of courage too, and I find it afresh in the thought of your dear affection for me. Farewell again. Never forget I shall always be your closest friend. H. R.

N.B. — Give our mother your news of me, I beg. Here is my exact address. It is not necessary to prepay letters to ensure their being delivered: —

  Mdlle. R.,
   Château de Clémensow,
    Poste de Zwierziniec,
     near Zamosc, Poland.

VI

Mdlle. Renan, *Château de Clémensow, Zwierziniec, near Zamosc, Poland.*

My Dear Henriette, — You will forgive my long silence when you know its motive. Since last we talked together many things have happened, things that in so peaceful a life as mine may well pass for events, and which render your counsels even more urgently necessary than before. Never have I realised the misfortune of being parted from my own people so bitterly as in the moments of perplexity whose story I will now comfort myself by telling you. Oh! how often and how enviously have I looked back upon those happy days when my troubles never lasted long, seeing I could end them once for all by confiding them to you. Now is the time, my dearest Henriette, when your presence and your counsel would indeed be useful to me. Is it fate, kind Heaven, that wills us never to appreciate our blessings till we have lost them? With the close of my stay at Issy came the moment fixed by the custom of that house for the tonsure of those deemed worthy of the rite, and I was among those called upon by our Superiors to take this first step in the sacerdotal path. This was no order, you must understand, not even a suggestion; it was simply a permission, whereof each was to avail himself or not, according to his own conclusions and the counsels of his Director. You may perhaps conceive, but I can never express, all the doubts and perplexities into which such a proposal naturally plunged me. I do not believe myself to have either exaggerated or dissimulated the importance of the step I had to consider. The engagement suggested was not an irrevocable one; it was no vow, but it was a promise — a promise based on honour and on conscience — a promise made to God Himself — and such a promise borders very closely on the nature of a vow. I felt, therefore, that I must meditate most deeply before making it, and my conscience cannot reproach me with having neglected any possible means of enlightenment.

I did not lack advice. God granted me a treasure as priceless as it is rare in the person of a remarkably kind and sagacious Director. In him I found a simplicity and truthfulness of character in perfect harmony with my own, and above all, a sensitive and practised tact, quick to understand and appreciate those shades of feeling which in such delicate matters can only be faintly indicated. At first his counsels tended towards an affirmative decision. Indeed, at one moment he was positive on the subject, but my temptations and doubts seemed to redouble their intensity in proportion to the earnestness I brought to bear on the all-important decision. And besides, the example of several of my comrades, who had settled to wait till they were at St. Sulpice, and had concluded their theological studies (the usual course of action), before giving their first pledge, was before my eyes. To be brief, all my previous difficulties crowded back upon my mind. Your advice, my own meditations, all added to my uneasiness. Truth compels me to acknowledge, indeed, that the idea of taking a backward step in the sacerdotal career never occurred to me. I never considered the matter except as a question of *delay*, and my Director strongly urged my taking no other view of it. But I could not conceal the fact that such a delay had become almost indispensable to me. At last the fresh considerations I submitted to him prevailed against his first opinion, and he informed me that, as no harm could be done by waiting, and some might possibly arise, in the present state of my mind, from undue precipitation, he would consent to the delay I asked for. "But in any case," he said, "keep the question in hand quite apart from that of your vocation for the priesthood. They are utterly and absolutely distinct, and you know my judgment as to the second of the two."

This, dearest Henriette, is a true history of what has come to pass. Perhaps you will think my conduct betrayed some irresolution. You must admit that if ever subject excused it, this one does. God will judge whether my motives have been tainted by inconstancy or thoughtlessness. My fault in the matter, if fault there is, lies here, that when it seemed about to take decisive form, I did perhaps mention it too positively to our mother, and I may have roused hopes she cherished, and which I have since been driven to dispel. That, I confess, has been much the tenderest point with me. I have had to summon all my courage to follow the voice of conscience rather than that of my own blood and its affections, in a business which I feared might cause sharp suffering to the most beloved of mothers. I gather from her letters that she has not been seriously affected. But the terrible dread I had of such an occurrence will be a great lesson to me for the future.

Finally, my dear Henriette, you may be surprised when I tell you that my views on the ecclesiastical state have never been so settled as since I have passed through this first ordeal. Never have I been so thoroughly convinced, never have my superiors so perfectly agreed in their assurances, that it is God's will that I should enter the priesthood. Not that I conceive it to be the ideal state of human happiness. Neither my knowledge of my own character nor my experience incline me to that opinion. But after all, dear Henriette, it is folly to amuse oneself running after a chimera when the thing itself has no existence here below. Duty, virtue, the gratification inseparable from the exercise of the noblest of our faculties, these are the only joys a man may reasonably seek for. Enjoyment, in its widest sense, is not for him, and he only wears himself out by fruitlessly pursuing it. Christianity once accepted, as it rationally may be, human existence has a different object. Nothing, to my mind, more conclusively attests the divine origin of the Christian theory of human life and happiness than the reproach so bitterly made against it by the modern schools, of forcing men to put themselves perpetually aside, to force back the tide, as it were, of their own natures, to set their happiness beyond the sphere of their own individuality and earthly pleasures. I can forgive the unbelievers freely enough, indeed, for not accepting Christianity. God makes the Christian, not himself, so that is only partially their fault. But I cannot forgive their failure to perceive that the Christian theory is merely the expression of a fact — the fact of the downfall and present misery of the human race. A simple practical study of mankind should have convinced them of this truth.

This point established, Christianity once proved and God's will manifested, as I have reason to believe it has been in my case, the logical consequence appears inevitable. One difficulty, however, has often preoccupied me. Even supposing, as I believe, that the fear of losing some comforts and of undergoing possible and considerable trouble is not a sufficient reason for drawing back, might not — so I have said to myself — the desire of preserving that sweet liberty and honest independence so necessary to the free action of the moral and intellectual faculties excuse me from embracing a career which, as I cannot conceal from myself, will give me but small opportunity of enjoying them?

Here is my answer. There are two kinds of intellectual freedom. One is bold, presumptuous, carping at all reverence. That kind of freedom is forbidden me by my priestly office, and even were I to embrace a different life, my conscience and my sincere love of truth would still forbid it me. So there can be no question of that sort of independence in my case.

There is another kind, wiser, respecting all things worthy of respect, despising neither persons nor beliefs, inquiring calmly and straightforwardly, using the reason God has bestowed because it was given for that purpose, never accepting nor rejecting any opinion on merely human authority. This is a freedom permitted to all men, and why not to a priest? It is true he has a duty in the matter beyond that of others — the duty of knowing when to hold his peace and keep his thought in his own heart; for those who take alarm at what they cannot comprehend are legion. But after all, is it such a trial to think for oneself alone, and is it not a secret spring of vanity which makes one so eager to communicate one's thoughts to others? Must not every man who desires to live in peace make to himself that law of silence of which I have just spoken? "We must have a hindmost thought," says Pascal, "and judge all things by it, yet must we speak as do the people."

This, too, is what the learned Director I have already mentioned to you impressed on me, laying such stress upon the point as to seem to speak out of his own experience. "Dear friend," he said, "if I did not know you to have the power of keeping silence, I would beseech you *not* to enter the priesthood." "Sir," I replied, "I have examined myself, and I think I can answer for possessing it."

Here, then, dearest Henriette, is the true story of my present position. It is an unspeakable consolation to me to know that in your heart, at all events, I shall always have a refuge where I may find that independence one so rarely meets with outside one's own. I take it as a quite special sign of His divine beneficence that God should have given man the enjoyments and familiar confidence of family life to compensate for the constraints necessarily imposed upon him by society. I often find great delight in dreaming of those ancient times when the family constituted the only social bond. We have made great progress since those days—so people say. Truly progress is a very relative term!

I find a somewhat less hazy consolation in the thought that I shall soon be enjoying the company of my good old mother and of our dear Alain. I do not think I have ever longed so earnestly to see them. The plan of our journey is already made out. It is settled that I am to go straight to Tréguier, and that towards the end of my vacation we are to move, my mother and I, to St. Malo. Mother will stay on there some time after my departure. Will this lead to a more permanent reunion? I should dare to hope it, did not the very prudent views expressed in your last letter make me hold my expectations concerning so delicate a business rigorously in check.

It will be an experiment, at all events, an indispensable preliminary, as you justly indicate, to any such arrangement.

You have doubtless heard of the excellent transaction Alain has just concluded, by which he undertakes to carry on M. Lemonnier's business operations. Though I am far from being in a position to appreciate its results, I fancy they will be very advantageous to him.

My dearest Henriette, pray calm the fear a passage in your last letter has aroused in me. You seemed to indicate — at all events, I fancied I understood — that the family in which you are employed is careless as to the repayment of the immense sacrifices you have made for it, and that you had to fight hard to secure that private independence which is the dearest treasure of existence. Oh, my Henriette! can it be thus your services are requited? Is this the reward of your exile? Tell me everything, I do beseech you. Use no more reserve in disclosing your troubles to me than I do in confiding mine to you. I shall suffer less, knowing their sad reality, than fancying, as I now do, that you are secretly nursing a sorrow which must be all the bitterer because it presupposes a most shameful ingratitude in those to whom your life has been devoted. That has been my worst fear. Oh, if it should prove true! Reassure me, I entreat you. Alain has forwarded me two hundred francs for my travelling expenses, and my mother tells me of a still larger sum you have sent to renew my wardrobe. Must everything fall on you? Poor Henriette! How can I ever repay all I owe you? God knows the chief sacrifice I offer Him in devoting myself to His service lies in renouncing the hope, not of repaying you indeed, but of doing so to anything like the extent you deserve. My love must supply what else is lacking.

I shall start between the 20th and 28th of July. So, if you calculate your answer cannot reach me before that date, you had better send it to Brittany. Yet I would rather have it here. Do tell me whether there is any glimmer of a chance of your coming to France before many years are out, either in charge of your pupils, or with their whole family, or otherwise? You mentioned such a possibility before you left us, and I often think of it. Tell me if it is nothing but a dream.

Farewell, my dear, good Henriette! Seeing the sole consolation of this earthly life is to love and to be loved, let us love each other unreservedly, and let us hope. Hope is always a happiness, and often it is bravery as well. May this thought sustain us! I can never know hopeless sorrow, for my part, so long as I have your affection to lean on. May you realise how fondly I requite it! E. RENAN.

VII

MDLLE. RENAN, *Zamoysky Palace, Warsaw, Poland.*

PARIS, *November* 27, 1843.

It is with great delight, my dearest Henriette, that I take up the thread of our intercourse, interrupted during the last few months by the moves from place to place which have broken the usual monotony of my life. My departure from Issy, my journeys to Tréguier and St. Malo, my settling down at St. Sulpice, have all left vivid, though very various, impressions on my mind. Now I am back at last in the ordinary channel of my existence, let me spend a moment in going over the past with you, dear Henriette, and try to give you some notion of my present condition of mind. You are the only living being, probably, to whom I can confide it wholly, without a shadow of concealment. My stay at Tréguier, dearest sister, was a time of perfect happiness to me. In all truth, I sorely needed it. My close and serious work during the two years I spent at Issy, the lack of a holiday the year before — for I do not count the weeks spent there in absolute solitude as being a real holiday — and above all, the severe trouble I went through at the close of my second year, had so broken me down, physically and morally, that I was unrecognisable. I almost frightened all our friends, and they have astonished me not a little by inquiring if I was quite recovered from *my illness*. You know how fruitful that country is in hypotheses, especially as to other people's affairs! However, my good mother's care of me has quite restored my health, and the happiness of being with her scattered, for the time, at all events, the anxieties which had haunted me so long. Indeed, I do not think I ever spent two happier months, and all the more so from their contrast with the preceding ones.

I led a pleasant, tranquil life, admirably suited to my tastes; I met with frank and honest friendship; I had the joy, always a keen one to me, of seeing my beloved Brittany once more; and above all, I sunned myself in that maternal love, so fond, so watchful, so devoted, which resembles no other affection, and of which our mother is the very pattern. I scarcely left her side during those two months. I was never so happy as with her, because nowhere else did I meet such confidence, such simplicity, and such truth. I was delighted, dearest Henriette, with her condition in every way. Her health is as good as we have any right to expect at her age, and considering the life she has led. She has a natural courage and cheerfulness which enable her to bear her loneliness perfectly, and indeed she receives every sort of attention from our own relations and all her neighbours. It is a real joy to me to have seen all this with my own eyes, and to feel I may be perfectly easy about her. I am convinced she could not be better off anywhere, once granting that she must be parted from her children.

Now, dearest Henriette, I come to my own personal concerns, and I will begin by saying a few words about the new house where I am settled. It is not very like those I have already passed through. The rule is broader and more general than at Issy. All that there smacked of the educational establishment is eliminated here; and indeed we are all of us young men of between twenty and thirty, most of whom have finished our ecclesiastical studies, and are working on our own account. Hence each, as it were, lives his life apart. The tone among the pupils is very good. There is perfect politeness, together with a striking air of coolness and mutual indifference. The huge majority come up from the provinces to spend a year or two, and care little about making acquaintances whom they are never likely to meet again. So the life is really a private one. Besides, there are so many of us, that we hardly see each other oftener than once in two or three months.

Hence you may judge how rare any amount of intimacy must be. You may imagine, too, that so large a company must be very *mixed*. This is true enough; yet the spirit of evil, of intrigue, of envy is kept under, at all events, if not utterly stifled.

Life here has not that quality of monotony which makes Issy so unendurable to those who have no taste for meditation. For my part, I am rather inclined to complain on the score of dissipation, and if there is one thing about Issy which I regret, it is the sweet if somewhat melancholy calm caused by the small number of the pupils and the quiet of the place. As for the Principals, their attention and care is admirable; but one feels it is all mechanical, that they are men who have been in the habit of doing the same thing for the next-comer for the last twenty or thirty years, and look on you merely as another pupil committed to their charge, never giving a thought to your personal individuality. But on the whole, the number of learned and distinguished men collected here surprises me. There is not a single member of the teaching staff who has not real merit, and some of them are remarkable alike for their talents and their erudition. The lectures are very carefully prepared and delivered, and are much more complete as to the instruction they impart than those in any other ecclesiastical establishment; in short, nothing which could possibly facilitate our studies is neglected. In material matters, everything is perfect. The cleanliness approaches luxury, though that is kept within reasonable bounds.

As to study, the only one practised here, strictly speaking, is Theology in all its various departments, canonical law, Scriptural history, and so forth. Hebrew is the only branch of knowledge, apart from Theology, in which a special course is given.

Theology has two very distinct sides, as far removed from each other in their object as in their method, and towards which I feel very differently inclined. One is what I should be disposed to call the demonstrative or apologetic side, which establishes the general principles and proofs of religion and of the doctrines of the Church. The second — what I should denominate the expository side — takes the first for granted, and explains the decisions and dogmas defined by the Church or contained in Scripture. The first of these two sides is grand and noble. It is a real philosophy, necessitating an analysis of mankind, of society, of critical discussions of all kinds, which, in a word, forces one into practical research. It is bound up with the highest questions which have occupied the human mind, and seems to me indispensable to any thinking man.

The case with regard to the other aspect of theological study is very different. Nothing indeed can be deeper than the dogmas which form its subject; but in that very fact the root of the evil lies. The human mind has lost itself in the endeavour to fathom such mysteries. Its efforts to class and submit to its own judgment matters belonging to an order of things totally beyond its comprehension have only ended in unfathomable subtleties of reasoning and unintelligible explanations. Such is the real character of this second department of Theology. It is permeated with the spirit of Mediæval Scholasticism, and still modelled, as it were, on its empty and abstract formulas. Happily form cannot affect the heart of any matter. Dogmatic Theology without Scholasticism has existed, and there is no reason why it should not emancipate itself once more. Nothing proves this possibility more thoroughly than the truth and beauty which mark the apologetic department of Theology. This, founded entirely on fact and induction, yet astounds one by its depth. For one of the greatest evidences of Christian truth, to my mind, is that its reality has to be demonstrated by the analysis of all the deepest feelings of mankind. There lies its key. If, on the other hand, Christianity were a delusion, such an analysis could not fail to overthrow it.

To my theological studies I have added that of

Hebrew, over which I expect to spend the greater part of my working hours. We have an excellent Hebrew professor, a profound scholar, abreast of all the additions modern science has made to that branch of learning. He has several times mentioned the name of a Mons. Latouche, of whom I fancy I have heard you speak. I have his work on Hebrew grammar, and I have looked into his general method. His principles seem to me correct, but, as far as I can judge, he is too hot-headed a person to be equal to constructing a scientific edifice. Though all his principles, as I have already stated, are true in substance, they are pushed too far. But some of his views, at all events, are excellent, and he possesses a most unusual amount of acuteness and a huge power of observation and of generalisation. This is the Professor's opinion as well as mine. The textbook for our Hebrew lessons is a French abridgment of the famous Grammar by Gesenius. Here again the Germans bear off the palm. They have turned the study of Hebrew into a real and rational *science*, as accurate as geometry, wherein memory plays but a subordinate part. The difficulties are far from great, however, when once one grows accustomed to the curious manner of writing the vowels, and to the variety of sounds given to the same letter. And indeed the knowledge of Hebrew leads up to such important linguistic rules, and it is so indispensably necessary to the due comprehension of the most ancient and remarkable, not to say the most venerated, of all books, that nobody could grudge the labour necessary to acquire it.

You will be surprised, perhaps, at my beginning to learn another language so soon after taking up German, in which I have made so little progress. Here is the truth, if it must be confessed. You know that when I began German I was short of money, and I had to sponge on other people's books, *i.e.*, instead of buying my own grammar, dictionary, explanatory works, &c., I borrowed them from one of my fellow-students, who had made great progress in the language. But, to my misfortune, he departed, taking his books with him. So I had to give up German for a season. When I got to St. Sulpice, I might have begun it again, but as I have the advantage here of a special course of Hebrew lectures, remarkable both for clever treatment and careful delivery, you will readily understand my preferring them to going on with a language I should have had to study alone as best I could.

Space fails me, dearest Henriette, and I have said nothing yet about the solemn reflections which fill my mind whenever it is not absorbed by study. You can easily guess their subject. Fresh though not imperative hints about taking that first step were given me almost as soon as I had entered this establishment. They have brought back all my doubts and anxieties. During the vacation my sole chance of happiness had lain in my rigid determination not to dwell on them. It is now my duty to examine the matter afresh, however painful it may be. Great Heaven! how cruel it is that a question so deeply affecting a man's whole existence must perforce be decided in such early youth. But that, my dearest Henriette, is a quite inevitable necessity, and must be submitted to, whatever line I may take up. For could I avoid it, even were I to renounce the ecclesiastical state? No, indeed; the matter must be settled one way or another, but a decision there must be, and the word itself is terrible to me.

If I could do aught to avoid it I would seize the chance; but I see none. It is a merciless dilemma. An abyss yawns on my right hand and on my left. Never did I realise the power of Providence over human destiny as when I perceived how little man himself is able to control the act which most affects his own fate. For I cannot conceal from myself the fact that all my meditation can serve but little to guide me, seeing the future, which alone could give me a fixed point for my inquiry, is mercilessly hidden from my view. True indeed it is that we are *led*. Happily the Christian may add, "We are *well led!*" This is indeed our only true and logical consolation. To conclude, my ideas have undergone but little change. Things in themselves, abstractions drawn from facts, *a priori* reasoning, attract me, but actual experience terrifies me. My own reflections, and the facts I daily witness, only confirm these two antagonistic tendencies of my nature. Will you believe that I can already appeal to personal experience in this particular? Did space permit it, my dear Henriette, I could tell you various things which would convince you my fears are not imaginary, and that if I do persevere I shall do it by sacrificing myself. Suffice it to say that envy and small-mindedness did much to embitter my last month at Issy. Fortunately the final advantage was mine before my own conscience, and even in the sight of men.

Farewell, my dearest Henriette! I expect to hear from you very shortly. The dates mentioned in Mdlle. Ulliac's[1] make me think letters get here more quickly from Warsaw. So I shall be on the watch a day or two hence. Oh, if you knew the happiness those letters of yours give me! They are epochs in my life.

---

[1] Mdlle. Ulliac Trémadeure, a devoted friend of Mdlle. Renan's. Her name is mentioned in "My Sister Henriette."

Farewell, once more. You know how boundless is the confidence and how deep the affection of your
ERNEST.

VIII

MDLLE. RENAN, *Zamoysky Palace, Warsaw, Poland.*

PARIS, *April* 16, 1844.

MY DEAR GOOD HENRIETTE, — I snatch a moment from the study and meditation which absorb me to rest and talk a little with you. Never has the need of such sweet intercourse seemed so intense as after these six long months of an isolation which would seem intolerable to any one unaware of the extent to which habit and a man's deliberate determination to rule his own mind will inure him to the most disagreeable conditions of existence. Conceive that since I said good-bye to our dear mother, that interchange of true and disinterested affection which our poor hearts so imperiously crave has existed for me in your and her letters only! Never one of those precious talks in which two hearts meet and comprehend one another without the cumbrous medium of artificial forms and borrowed language. Of the people who surround me, some (few, luckily, in number) are not worthy either of my friendship or my confidence; the others, stranded here for a time, have either given their affections elsewhere, or possess none at all, and care little for the stranger chance has set beside them, who will be a stranger to them to the end of time. Imagine one of those ancient Roman walls which, one is told, is built of stones laid one on the other without any mortar between them. There you have an exact image of the house in which I am spending a considerable portion of those years which the world assures us are the fairest of our lives. Local contiguity is the only bond uniting these often incongruous elements, drawn together by views as various in their origin.

And thus it is to you, my dearest Henriette, and to our beloved mother, that my thoughts tend, as though by their own weight, the moment they are free to turn whither affection calls them. How often, in the midst of arduous labour and abstruse study, have I caught myself wandering in that Poland of which you draw such a melancholy picture, but which I cannot help fancying beautiful and smiling when I remember it holds the object of my love! How often, too, I have fancied myself between you and my mother, the happiest trio! Nature, perforce, fills up the emptiness of reality by dreams. Would you believe, dear Henriette, that for an instant I thought mine were going to come true? About a month ago I had a letter from our dear mother, and you may conceive my astonishment and joy at reading these words:— "Henriette tells me she is coming to France; we hope to arrange so that she will be here during your vacation," &c., &c. The most admirable plan, in a word, that could have been invented. Even the dates and the length of your stay had been made out.

Such a brilliant plan, so unexpected, so sudden, astounded me, and as you may well believe, it coincided too closely with my dearest wishes for me to hesitate much as to believing in it. I did so believe in it, and I began to make plans of my own — to improve on our poor mother's dreams even. That sort of thing is catching, so it seems. Yet I could not help feeling occasional twinges of doubt. Supposing our good mother had been paying more heed to her own desires than to the strict meaning of the letter. Supposing she had turned the expression of a wish into an assertion. The possibility alarmed me all the more, because, looking at the project in the light of my past recollections, I could not but feel it all too unlikely.

Another letter came at last, and proved my fears were only too well founded. "Alas! my dear Ernest," wrote my dear mother, "I misunderstood that passage in Henriette's letter. Madame Gaugain has pointed out to me that the whole thing depends on whether the family decides on coming to France or not." What a disappointment, my poor Henriette! It has so disheartened me that I have a mind to give up building castles in the air for ever.

By a singular coincidence, your last letter reached me on the very day — I had almost said at the very hour — when, after long and painful doubt, I took my first formal step in the ecclesiastical career. Two days previously I was still in a state of overwhelming uncertainty. Neither my mother, nor anybody in the world except the person with whom I was bound to confer on the subject, knew anything of it. I should merely repeat what I have so often described were I to attempt to reproduce the thoughts and impressions which passed through my mind concerning this all-important decision. I only made it because I perceived that not doing so meant making the very opposite one, which was still more distasteful to me. So I had to make up my mind to it, all the more so because the engagement I was called upon to contract has no irrevocable character either in God's sight or man's. It is no more than an expression of a present intention, leaving the future free. And that present intention I conscientiously entertain. Besides, I say again, to have shrunk afresh from so undecisive a forward step would have been tantamount, under the circumstances, to taking a very decided backward one; though at the same time I can honestly affirm that I did not obey any exterior influence whatever. After all, in vowing my life to God, and to what I hold to be His truth — in taking that truth for the portion of my inheritance (the literal words I used in my profession), in renouncing all vanity and superfluity, all foolish delights, and what are known as pleasures — I only do what I have always unflinchingly desired to do. Any hesitation I have felt has arisen from my not being certain what *was* truth, and whether that truth demanded that I should serve the Church, in spite of the personal difficulties I could not help foreseeing. But whether I entered the priesthood or not, nay, more, whatever my feelings as to the religion in which I believe I have found the truth may ultimately be — a grave and quiet life, retired from luxury and pleasure, would always be my choice. I have promised nothing beyond that, and such a promise seems to me the necessary preamble to any really serious pursuit, the indispensable preliminary to a life devoted to virtue and to truth.

If I had been the leader of a school of philosophers, I would have imposed a ceremony on my disciples, the very counterpart of that which the Church has instituted for the first stage of ecclesiastical consecration, because the whole spirit of that ceremony is summed up in the renunciation of all that is neither good, nor true, nor noble, and apart from such renunciation philosophy cannot exist. If ever I become a vain and frivolous man, clinging to the despicable treasure that must pass away, or to a public opinion more despicable still (I do not speak of glory, which is no vanity, when properly understood), then indeed I shall know I have failed to keep my vow.

I have thought a great deal, my dear Henriette, over the suggestions contained in your last letter as to my accepting some position which would give me an opportunity for foreign travel before definitely settling down into the ecclesiastical life. You may imagine that, while unable to make an immediate decision on such an important point (though it could not take immediate effect in any case), I greatly value the hope of making use of such an opportunity at some future time. I feel with you that nothing is more likely to give one an insight into men and things, and to form those reasoning powers which must be rooted in experience and in contact with mankind. Not, indeed, I confess, that I believe myself destined to be a man of action, properly so called: I fancy the world of thought is much more likely to be my domain. But, nevertheless, I hold that even in that respect foreign travel, occasional, if not habitual, confers a great and inestimable advantage by raising the traveller's mind above that narrow partial prejudice which, as it were, forcibly imprisons the man who has never breathed any intellectual atmosphere save that of his own country.

Yet I often ask, as I think of the future most congenial to my tastes, whether the years still at my disposal would not be best employed in further study. In my present state of mind I dare not answer positively. This fact will make you feel how determined I am not to prejudice the liberty I reserve to myself of making some future decision in the matter. In any case, nothing can happen for the next eighteen months, for I want to spend the whole of next year at St. Sulpice, so as to push forward my theological studies and perfect myself in Hebrew, for which special facilities are here offered.

It is more than likely that I may be invited to spend several years at St. Nicolas as a teacher. The offer might indeed come very shortly; but though the plan has some advantages, on other accounts I only half desire it. I love and esteem M. Dupanloup as a man for his qualities of head and heart. He unites remarkable acuteness with a generosity and nobility of feeling rare enough now-a-days. But he is well known to be one of the most imperious natures on the face of the earth, though certain very sharp discomforts which he has lately endured in consequence of this failing may have given him a profitable lesson, if indeed such a fault as his be curable. And besides, the greater number of the teaching staff of that establishment are afflicted with a small-mindedness which borders on love of tittle-tattle, and which would not at all suit me. Nevertheless, as I should never set myself up to dispute M. Dupanloup's management of his own seminary, and as the second drawback can always be avoided, as far as interior influences go, by keeping oneself to oneself, I should not object to spending one or two years there, so as to have an opportunity of attending certain lectures and pursuing certain researches which can only be conveniently made in Paris; after which, my dream would be to bury myself in the depths of Brittany with my mother for a while, so as to ruminate in peace over the facts I shall have collected, and to ripen certain ideas in my brain. The researches *must* be made in Paris, I think, and the result *must* be thought over and elaborated amidst a silence and calm which I should never find in greater perfection than in our little home with my poor, dear mother. Besides, this plan would give both her and me a certain period of happiness. But you will understand, my dearest Henriette, that I am too well aware of our position to dare to look at the realisation of this last point in any light but that of a desire, or at the utmost of a very distant hope; yet it has long been an element in every plan of mine. What dreams, dear Henriette, and how foolish we should be did we not laugh at them even while we dream them!

As to the more distant future, it often beckons me, I must confess, but I make a rule never to allow it to preoccupy my thoughts. Yet it seems to me useful to glance at it from time to time, so as to regulate the march towards one's appointed end. Well, I already hold some important facts which convince me I need not be drawn against my inclinations into a sphere of occupation unsuited to my tastes and intellectual needs. The chief of these is the strong opinion expressed by my superiors as to my qualifications and the tendency of my character, which opinion, as you may fancy, has a decided influence on my future. They have frequently and formally assured me, and I had previously assured myself, that the priestly office in its ordinary sense, what I might call parochial duty, would in no way suit my turn of mind. But, you may say, beyond that particular line there is nothing left a priest to do except to teach; and teaching in general, especially in the case of an ecclesiastic, does not offer a smiling prospect, *under present circumstances*. That is true, dear Henriette; yet I think some happy medium may perchance be found between that ministry to which God certainly has not called me, and the thorny career of the professional teacher. Without being able exactly to define it, I think I at least perceive a possibility of such a thing. The Archbishop of Paris is even now engaged in ripening a great plan — that of founding a college for advanced study, with a curriculum so high-class and so extended as to satisfy every taste. My present Principal, a man of considerable merit, is to be one of the chief pillars of the new institution, and several times, when I have expressed my fear of being set to do work quite out of harmony with my tastes, he has given me indirect hints that he would see there should be an opening for me if I desired it. But I confess I should be very fastidious, and I should insist on being permitted a close and careful preliminary study of the spirit and constitution of the establishment. In any case, one last resource is open to me — to enter the Society of St. Sulpice for a few years, at all events. There I am *sure* of being received with open arms, as is proved by the tolerably explicit proposals already made me thence, which I have thought it best not to notice so far. As this congregation only deals with the great seminaries, the duties are not so irksome as where elementary and classical teaching is required. But I would not join it except on the express condition of never being employed outside the diocese of Paris, and I should do so with the full intention of leaving it in the course of a few years, as do most of the priests who enter it. For although the body is known as a society, in its case, as in that of its pupils, juxtaposition is the sole bond of fellowship. Its members make neither engagements nor promises. If this were not so, I would not have anything to do with it for all the world. I am steadfastly bent on preserving the hope of some day being able to lead that solitary and retired life which, granted a small circle of true friends, has such a charm for any one capable of thought or feeling. Oh, dearest Henriette! then indeed your presence will become an indispensable element in my happiness! You are the being God has given me to love, and to love me, with that pure affection which is Nature's true gift, and therefore that of Providence. I have told you all my idle dreams. Who else should know them but the dear confidant of my inmost thoughts, she who, with one other person only, fills a heart God has blessed with such great power to love. However things fall out, my chief desire, for the sake of which I am prepared for any sacrifice, to which I shall ever cling, though that should call for superhuman strength, is to preserve those principles of uprightness and honesty which ensure true happiness apart from chance events and human struggle.

I had a letter from our good mother very lately. She is well, and cheerful, and contented, still living, as she has always lived, in us and for us. She is already rejoicing, poor dear soul, at the thought of having me back with her before many months are out. You may fancy the idea makes me as happy as her. But it pains me, dear Henriette, I confess, to feel your labour and your exile pay the price of our enjoyment. The thought casts a kind of shadow on my happiness. When will you cease to be the only one of us that does not benefit by your own work?

Farewell, my dearest Henriette! I thank Heaven for giving me your love in compensation for my many troubles. The confidence I can repose in you consoles me amply for the inevitable reserve and silence of my daily life — I count the days that must go by before you can receive this long effusion of mine, and try to calculate how soon I may expect your answer. You may fancy how much I long for it. Farewell, once more. He who inspired my love for you alone can realise how deep it is.

ERNEST RENAN,
Cl. T.[1]

---

[1] "Clerc tonsure" — tonsured clerk.

IX

WARSAW, *May* 9, 1844.

I have been reading your letter over again, and kissing it, my dearest dear beloved brother: that letter I had longed for so earnestly, and welcomed with such intense delight! Alas! my Ernest, too true it is that life, in many a case at least, has to be spent among people with whom no intercourse beyond the coldest civility is possible — and neither you nor I are likely to be satisfied with that. Heaven grant that your experience of a life which must be hard and trying for many years, in any case, — and to which some men never can grow accustomed, — may be but temporary! Already I keep reckoning up the months yet to elapse before you see our dear mother again, and hail the approach of that moment as joyfully as she can herself. To know you two happy is the greatest satisfaction I can feel.

I hopelessly wonder, dearest Ernest, what passage in any letter of mine can have given our mother the idea of the fair dream you mention, and concerning which she too has written me. No more delightful plan could be devised, but none, alas! could, at this moment, be less practicable. You may rely on this, my dear boy, I never could have mentioned any date to our mother, seeing I have no right to nurse the smallest reasonable hope of the kind she means.

Courage, patient waiting, resignation, must still be our cry. Far from moving homewards, I am just about starting off again in the very opposite direction. We are leaving Warsaw for the lonely country house where I have already spent two summers; and though it is only sixty leagues from here, my heart is heavy at the thought of turning my back on Western Europe and on all I hold most dear. My letters, too, are always greatly delayed in transit there, which is a severe trial to me. Except for these two causes, I shall regret nothing at Warsaw. My life here is as quiet as it is in the country, and indeed, since I have been in Poland, I have grown perfectly indifferent as to what spot I live in. I never meet a congenial soul in any of them. In consequence of this departure, I must ask you, my Ernest, to direct all letters in future thus:

Mdlle. R.,
Château de Clémensow,
Zamosc, Poland.

Will you be good enough to give the same instructions to our mother and to Alain, for I feel very uneasy about any letters which might arrive here, after our departure. Nothing can exceed the uncertainty of the postal arrangements in this country.

Our brother had already told me, very briefly, dear

Ernest, that you had resolved upon the preliminary engagement you also mention in your letter. I have no right to cavil at it, my poor dear boy, nor yet to advise you on the steps still lying before you; my first duty, and my chief desire, are to leave you perfectly free in every decision you may have to make. Why, oh, why must they be taken at an age when you must still perforce be so inexperienced in life's difficulties? You will have observed, my dear, if you read my last letter over again, that the prospect of travel indicated to you was very distant, and that, indeed, I rather suggested an idea than pointed out a course of action. So it will always be, my dear boy. I shall tell you anything I think worth your consideration, and you will be perfectly free to decide afterwards as you think best. I have never had any opinion of advisers who take it ill if their counsels are not followed.

The idea of your accepting a professorship at St. Nicolas, at your early age, does not recommend itself to me. To make such a position at all advantageous, it should carry some special facilities for continuing your advanced studies. Failing that, what would you gain by accepting the wearisome duties of an usher, or even by taking an elementary Latin class? Would it not be a pity thus to spend time which might be so much more usefully employed? Your idea of going into our native province and ripening the fruits of your studies in solitude, is by no means impracticable. If God grants me life and health, and His divine support, you will find me only too glad to second this and any other project of yours.

It is futile, perhaps, to try to look into the more distant future. Circumstances may alter that so much! But let me beseech you, my poor boy, never to join any society which would destroy your liberty of action, thus denying you the enjoyment of your own intellect, and parting you from those who love you. Never forget that by the very act of joining any such association you abdicate all right of personal judgment; and you will frequently find yourself forced into some action for the corporate body, which, as a private individual, you never would have attempted. It would be the bitterest sorrow in my life to see you forced into a line unnatural to you, and driven to take part in squabbles which, I feel and hope, your desire would be always to avoid. Dearest Ernest, do calm my saddened heart by often telling me you are resolved to keep your spirit pure and upright, that no man shall ever shake it, and that should Heaven be pleased to reunite us I shall still find you the brother I have loved so fondly, and whom I shall cherish to my life's end.

Do me a *learned* service, dear brother! Will you

kindly write me out a list of the chief Greek and Latin historians, with the period each of them covers, and send it to me as soon as you can do so, without inconvenience or fatigue. I have read several (in translations, of course), but I fear I may have overlooked some important authors, and I rely on you to remedy my mistake. Do not let this request astonish you, dear Ernest; alone and unaided, I have been forced to fill many a gap in my original education, and alone, too, I have had to fit myself for my present great undertaking. After a considerable amount of historical study, I have fallen back on its original sources, the genuine classics, like any lower-form schoolboy. Nothing daunts me, when the advantage of the young minds I have to cultivate, the accomplishment of the duty confided to me, comes in question. And indeed, spending so much time alone as I do, study is my great consolation, — the only one left me, perhaps, in this country where habits, tastes, and social condition, everything, in fact, differs so utterly from my home surroundings. Often I feel I would prefer to live entirely in my own room and my pupils' schoolroom. But that, unluckily, is not always possible, although I do often take advantage of the reputation for oddity my love of solitude has earned me. I could not make up my mind to waste my time as I see those around me waste it, nor spend long hours in futile vapid talk.

I feel my letters often betray this peculiarity of mine. I tell you scarcely anything about outside things. First of all because I am forced to be very circumspect in that particular, and also because I cannot fancy your finding any interest in descriptions of the Cossacks of every shape, and Orientals of every shade, who pass incessantly before my sight. Sometimes, in the winter, as I watched long files of sledges passing the gates of this splendid house, I used to find myself wondering whether I could really be living in the same hemisphere as before. That doubt has often struck me since. Fortunately for me, I have made up my mind to pay no attention to anything beyond what affects the advancement of my pupils' education. Nothing else has any interest for me. To serve those I love, devote all my power to them, pour out my affections on them, these are the mainsprings of my life, the objects always foremost in my mind, and which I follow with equal keenness under every sky. Have no anxiety about me, my Ernest; personal matters very seldom affect me. Forgive this disjointed letter. I finish it on the very eve of our departure, and amidst all the confusion consequent upon it. At least it will prove the unchangeableness of my love for you, and my constant eagerness to express it.

I hope you will write before the vacation opens.

Tell me when it begins, and how long you will be able to stay with our poor, dear mother. Every one who sees her confirms what your letter tells me of her excellent state of health. You will believe that nothing short of this unanimity of opinion could still an anxiety which must be endured to be appreciated. Her own letters, too, are calm and even joyful, when she has a hope of soon seeing you again. She tells me she is to go and await you at St. Malo. Farewell, my dearest Ernest. Be sure the confidence and affection your letter breathes have cheered and strengthened my heart. You know they fall on no ungrateful ground, and that the dearest affection of your sister, your true friend, is yours for ever.

H. R.

P.S.—I transmit this letter by the same means as I employed in sending you the last. Do not forget to let our mother and Alain know my address. You will kiss them for me, within two or three months from now!

X

Mdlle. Renan, *Chateau de Clémensow, near Zamosc, Poland.*

Paris, *July* 11, 1844.

Before I join our good mother, my dear excellent sister, I must have another talk with you. When these lines reach you, I shall, I think, be close on meeting her; for my departure is fixed for some day between the 20th and 25th of this month. The thought of it has absorbed me for some time. It is the natural centre-point of all my hopes and longings, whenever I allow them to follow their instinctive bent. A life of solitude has certain charms, no doubt, but stripped of all those sweet affections which feed the heart, and unduly prolonged as well, it is a cruel torture. Imagine that during the last ten months I have never seen one familiar face save those of the persons chance brought hither when I came myself. A poor sort of friendship that, born of a connection utterly devoid of mutual heart attraction!

I do not complain of the dearth of those uninteresting visitors who may suffice to the happiness of people the sole object of whose exterior intercourse is to get rid of themselves, and escape the weariness inseparable from their own personal reflections. I am thankful to be rid of them. But I do cruelly miss the visitors to whom the purest and most legitimate affection binds me — the delightful talks in which soul speaks to soul as though it spoke to itself — the kind of intercourse, in short, which God permitted me while gradually teaching me to live a kind of life to which I was a perfect stranger, and the trials of which I as yet ignored. But I am ashamed, my dearest Henriette, to talk of loneliness, when I remember that you bear it at its bitterest, without even that annual rest which breaks the usual tenor of my dreary life. I never think of the happiness I am shortly to enjoy without remembering that she to whom I owe it will herself be bereft of it, for years, it may be, yet. The thought pains me deeply, dearest Henriette, and my sole consolation is in hope, and in the consciousness of that affection which is the only true reward of such devotion as yours. Do you remember how you wept, five years ago, when I was leaving you to go and see our good old mother? I weep myself whenever I think of it! Poor Henriette! What shall we say now? Ah! that the thought of you will never leave us through the happy time now drawing near. Last year, it was on you that all our conversation turned.

I must tell you, my dear Henriette, that since last I wrote I have made another forward step in the ecclesiastical career. But it has not cost me the anxiety and hesitation which marked my first, of which it is, so to speak, the outcome. It adds neither bond nor obligation to those of my former condition, which in itself indeed entails nothing of that sort. Therefore no special scruple was called for. But in future the case will alter. The next step, now lying before me, is definite and irrevocable.[1] It is still in the dim distance fortunately; the strictly minimum period before taking it is a year, and that may be extended, I believe. I cannot think of it without terror, and when I remember my past anguish, I cry, "My God! my God! let this cup pass from me!" Nothing is so painful as doubt in a matter which must affect the whole of one's future life. Yet, "not my will, but Thine, be done!" You will support me, will you not, my Henriette? At all events by assuring me you love me!

There is one point, among the considerations for our future on which our last letters have touched, to which I desire to return; for I should not at all like you to misunderstand my real feelings concerning it. They are irrevocably fixed, and are as follows: When I expressed my inclination to a life of study and re-

[1] The subdeaconate.

tirement, in preference to one involving the exercise of the exterior functions of the priesthood, you seemed to fear I might seek to realise this project by joining some religious congregation or society. The thought alarmed you, and I can well understand it, for I assure you I am as averse as you can be to a manner of life which would absorb all my individuality into an abstract body. Such a body destroys, as you justly remark, all personal feeling, and forces its members to do in its service what they never would have dreamt of as private individuals. My opinion on the subject is a very strong one, I repeat, but I believe it to be quite correct. I am convinced that religious corporations, useful as they may be at certain periods, and to certain persons, are equally out of place in, and unsuited to, others. I am further convinced that the present is one of the periods, and I myself one of the individuals in question.

To my thinking, an honest searcher after truth must ever endeavour to elude a bondage which makes it his duty (or his necessity rather, for duty is quite another thing) to adhere to the doctrines of such and such a school, rather than to the truth his own reason recommends. Amidst the lively controversies now occupying public opinion in this country, and which I look on as part of the frivolous pabulum indispensable to those whose passions need some special stimulant — while recognising that the observer who is able to keep himself scornfully outside them may yet draw useful conclusions from them — amidst these controversies, I say, which I have carefully considered, I have succeeded in forming an opinion (on religious societies) as far removed from the frantic declamations of those who love to see mystery where none exists, as from the absurd panegyrics lavished by those small minds who see the type of sovereign perfection in a very human institution.

Both parties seem to me equally ignorant of the two great laws of human nature: 1st. That whoever thinks to find a human work — under whatever name, be it even that of Jesus Christ — whatever its avowed object, even the saintliest — whatever means, even the purest, serve its ends — in which the human passions, their influence and their action, have no share, seeks the impossible. 2nd. That whereas humanity eternally progresses, and such institutions remain stationary, it inevitably follows that those of one century must be out of harmony with the next, and that to attempt to keep them going is like trying to warm a corpse, and is a proof of extreme folly. Such is my idea, and its practical corollary is that I must hold myself absolutely aloof from the passionate and self-interested discussions so eminently distasteful to the faithful seeker after truth, who should never pay such follies the compliment implied by heated argument concerning them. Once they have died out, and I am dead, neither they nor I will have gained much by their absorption of that small modicum of calm which constitutes the chief charm of our little earthly span, and is so easily dissipated. Therefore I will keep clear of those empty controversies which only divert mankind from the true objects of existence, and never allow myself to be an interested party to any of them. But, my dear Henriette, I do not look on an aggregation of men brought together by a common object, and similarity of occupation, and only united in the bond of a purely temporary and voluntary propinquity, as a regular religious society. A man is not supposed to abdicate his liberty when he joins a teaching body, at a university, for instance. Well, I seek in vain for the symptom of any closer bond amongst the members of the societies to which I have alluded. No other, in fact, exists.

However, dear Henriette, certain events, the forerunners probably of other and more important ones, which have begun to shape themselves since my last letter to you, will probably and completely alter my future plans. I do not enlarge on them just now, for everything is still in a mere hearsay condition, as far as I am concerned, — and besides the fulfilment of the scientific commission you gave me, and which I send herewith, obliges me to be somewhat curt. The matter shall be the subject of our next talk on paper.

I beg you will forgive the confusion of the secondary paragraphs in the notes I send you. It was easy to keep to a fixed method, in dealing with the great historians. But with the cloud of lesser ones, I should have had to devote a large amount of time and care to a mere work of arrangement, which I felt your own clear-headedness would easily supply. May I ask you to do me a somewhat similar service? If you are on friendly terms with any learned ecclesiastic, would you find out from him what the *general teaching* is, in Polish schools, and those of neighbouring countries, on the following theological subjects: —

I. Are the Dogmatic Decrees of the Sovereign Pontiffs looked on as rules of faith, infallible and unchangeable by their own nature, or is the consent of the Universal Church necessary to give them this weight?

II. What is the Sovereign Pontiff's power with regard to the Canons of Discipline, and can he force any particular church to renounce its customs and its freedom?

III. In matters of doctrine and discipline, is the Pope superior to the Œcumenical Council or not?

IV. Has the Pope any authority, direct or indirect, over monarchs, in the *temporal* sense, and if not how are the various incidents during the Middle Ages, when such power was claimed, to be explained? Were they downright *usurpation*, or the outcome of the *public rights* which governed civil society at that period? I am anxious to discover whether the answers French theologians give these questions, which are known as the Gallic Doctrine, are really peculiar to themselves. The fact is very much contested just now, and I thought you might be able to throw some light on it. You understand, of course, that what I desire to know is the *teaching in the schools* and not the feeling of any private individual, nor the intrinsic value set by him on the doctrines set forth above. My question only relates to a matter of fact.

We must part, for the nonce, dear Henriette. I hope the happiness I shall have in our dear mother's society will be increased by hearing from you. I write to-day to say I shall be with her shortly. My sense of the mutual love which swallows up the miles between us, is my only consolation for the irreparable void your absence causes us.

Farewell, beloved Henriette. Think of the great love and tenderness for the best of sisters that fills your Ernest's heart.   E. RENAN.

XI

MDLLE. RENAN, *Château de Clémensow, Zamosc,
Poland.*

MY DEAR KIND HENRIETTE,—I too must send you a few words! How happy I have been since I wrote you those last lines from my usual place of residence! To embrace our darling mother; to look once again on scenes which never fail to rouse the tenderest association of ideas; to come back to those domestic habits which shed such powerful sweetness on the soul, softening and yet not enervating it—these joys were more than enough to cure the weariness caused by my usual mode of life, and to alter the somewhat severe cast of thought thereby induced. A mother's voice seems to have a peculiar power to soften everything, even when she intends it least. And where is pure and disinterested affection to be found save on one's mother's breast? It is but just, seeing how urgently man's heart needs it, that God should provide for each human being a refuge where he is sure to find what he would vainly seek elsewhere.

My mind has never been so clear as now. The intellectual faculties have some secret affinity with those of the affections and the moral powers, and rebound to every pressure which causes these last to suffer or rejoice. The two systems are meant to walk abreast, not to supply each other's place. Study, by feeding one's intelligence, may soften the suffering of one's starved affections. This is true enough, but the result is obtained by diverting the mind from their hunger, not by staying it. Thanks be to God, then, my dear Henriette, for having granted us this blessed rest, this balm for every ill!

I have called a truce with my dreams about the future. It is not that such thoughts never assail me, except in the course of my ordinary existence. I try then to master them, and not let them preoccupy me. But if they sometimes do come back on me here, they are more like dreams than thoughts. And there is no great harm in dreams, especially in vacation-time. I find our good mother in very good case. It is wonderful how she bears her loneliness, great as it is. She has the very happiest nature I have ever known. And her health seems to me very satisfactory. Her tender affection is the one great happiness of my holidays. I am very fastidious about the persons on whom I bestow my confidence and friendship, and the characteristics of my neighbours here do not tempt me to form fresh intimacies among them.

The neighbouring clergy, worthy as they are, are so limited in their views that I should fear any close or prolonged intercourse with them might end by making mine as narrow. There is one work only, as far as I can see, for which they are eminently fitted, and that is, to preach a crusade against the university. They would begin it to-morrow, I doubt not, if they could count with certainty on finding followers. However that may be, their enthusiastic and disinterested zeal is really comical. It amuses me vastly, and has given me opportunity for some curious physiological observations as to the manner in which human opinion is formed, and the guileless fashion in which simple-minded men blind themselves to their real motives.

The holiday task I have set myself is to carry on my Hebrew studies. What I did last year has enabled me to vanquish mere textual difficulties and to enjoy the beauty of that pure and ancient literature. I apply myself especially to its poetry, and above all to the Psalms, the most precious relics left us in that department. They are an inexhaustible source of admiration, and of scientific observation as well, to one who recognises them as the earliest childish song of the human race, and their language as that in which mankind lisped its first accents. From this point of view these ancient fragments are of priceless value, and if any psychologist were to endeavour to work out the theory of the faculty of spontaneous inspiration — the poets (one which has been less studied than almost any other) — here it is that his materials should be sought. For, to my thinking, this faculty was a childish one which only existed in the ancient world, and those who now call themselves poets merely imitate as to its form. But the thing itself, the poetic flame, is quenched utterly, and our poets are driven to assuring us they are inspired in splendid verse to hide their lack of genuine inspiration. Hence it is that, as Pascal says, honest folk see no distinction between a poet's work and an embroiderer's.

I hope for your answer both to these few lines, and to the letter I sent you on leaving Paris, before we leave for St. Malo. This will crown my holiday delights. I have left all business details to our mother. But we discuss them in leisurely fashion in our walks and talks. May they all end well! Farewell, my dear good Henriette! You know how few human beings share your Ernest's heart, and you know too how large a place in that heart you hold.

E. R.

XII

Mdlle. Renan, *Château de Clémensow, Zwierziniec, Zamosc, Poland.*

Paris, *December* 1, 1844.

I have put off writing for some time, my dear kind Henriette, because every day I have hoped for a letter from you. I fancied I recollected that in the last I received during my vacation you promised I should have a long one during the first days after I got back to the Seminary, early in November, that is to say. I must have been mistaken, for I have received nothing. As so often happens, I must have taken my own wishes for realities, and my yearning must have turned to hope. So I wait on from one post to the next, and the visiting hours, once so indifferent to me, now rouse my impatient interest, because I hope they may bring Mdlle. Ulliac's messenger, who has so often been the bearer of good news to me. I still hope he will come before long, but I will not further delay the pleasure of a quiet talk with you.

Well, I parted from our dear mother some six weeks since. I think I told you, dear Henriette, what a joy it was to me to find her health and

cheerfulness unaltered. With what delight did I
hear her contrast her latter years with the troubled
and sorrow-laden days of her former life, and attribute
the change under God to her beloved children!
Truly our mother is the most beautiful type of
motherhood I can conceive. She lives in us alone,
she identifies herself with us utterly. The only
difference I noticed in her this last visit was that
her loneliness seems to try her more than heretofore.
She never said so, but several little circumstances
made me draw that conclusion.

XIII

MDLLE. RENAN, *Château de Clémensow, Zwierziniec,
near Zamosc, Poland.*

PARIS, *December* 1, 1844.

. . . . . .

The quiet and calm in which I spent the holidays
has quite restored me from the state of exhaustion
into which I fell during the closing months of last
year. My health has never been better, and indeed
I am actually stronger now than when I returned.
Yet the first days were very trying. I was astonished
to find how painful the ordeal still was in spite of having gone through it so often before. A whole world

of sad and painful thoughts, bitter and anxious too, which had been slumbering within me began to stir once more. After a day or two, however, when I had settled down to work, my nerves grew calmer. Moreover, dearest Henriette, my position has undergone a change this year, which seems to me important. Not so much in itself as because of the influence I already perceive it may have upon my future. I have adverted to my Hebrew studies, and the fairly rapid progress I have made with them. In fact, though I have only been working at it for a year, our Hebrew professor, who finds the two sets of lectures given here simultaneously more than he can manage, has induced the principals to intrust one course to me.

I had no hesitation about agreeing to his proposal, as much for the sake of the scientific advantage it may bring me, as because I saw at once it might lead to something else. Besides, it is a principle of mine always to follow a path that seems to open up before me, seeing I cannot tell whither it may not lead me. Other people take my view, and those who have congratulated me have not failed to point out that the present Professor of Hebrew at the Sorbonne began in a precisely similar way. I have, indeed, already had a hint about a professorship, or rather an assistant-professorship (in the first instance), of the same language, in a sort of Theological Faculty just now projected by Monseigneur Affré, the Archbishop of Paris. But the plan appears so vague, both as to the time and manner of its execution, that I hardly know what to think of it. Yet I hear it said the College will certainly be open within a year. That remains to be seen. You will understand I have not definitely refused. If the position realised that which I conceive possible without daring to hope for it, it would ensure me the life of study and meditation I pine for, without forcing me to join a religious society, from which I so greatly shrink.

The professors, so I learn, would occupy an excellent position in every way. Without putting much confidence in this particular plan, I think I may certainly conclude from my present circumstances, from the opinions of my fellow-students and of my superiors, and from the reputation my success in my college career, reckoned somewhat remarkable, has brought me, that I may dismiss all fear as to the nature of my future life. And I feel protected from that too common danger of self-delusion by the fact that I have never known myself err on the side of optimism. In any case, let me repeat, I build no special hopes on this particular plan, of which indeed I am inclined to doubt, for several reasons. I confine myself to deducing certain possibilities from the fact of its suggestion.

I was not a little astonished when the Superior, in proposing I should undertake the duty I have mentioned, expressed a desire I should accept a pecuniary remuneration, in spite of the fact that I am still following the general course of study, and am not supposed to be anything more than an ordinary pupil. He first suggested a sum of two hundred francs. You may imagine how gladly I would have accepted, both on your account and mine. But his proposal was couched in a form which made me suspect that the society was willing to do this, and even more, for me, in the hope of my one day rendering it valuable service. And I know the same thing is being done in the case of others who do intend to join it.

This idea did not please me, and I carefully avoided giving any colour to such a supposition. With this object I refused to accept a fee. At last, pressed by the Superior, I consented to take a hundred francs, to cover the cost of several important books necessary to the proper preparation of my lectures. To strike the balance between us, he fixed the sum at a hundred and fifty francs; I preferred to sacrifice fifty, and accept what is given as a friendly acknowledgment of service rendered, rather than receive payment as a future member of the society. An implied promise, nay, even a cause for gratitude to any society alarms me, for the only way to prove such gratitude, it seems to me, would be to enroll oneself a member. It is better to refuse a benefit than to expose oneself to any risk of not being able to acknowledge it. I have taken your consent for granted. For indeed, dear Henriette, the matter, in a sense, concerns you more than me.

I too have begun to work seriously at my German this year. I have already made some progress, and a few days ago, following the universal custom, I began Lessing's Fables. On the whole, the queer construction of the language and the anomalies of its irregular verbs are the only real difficulties which strike me. I get much useful help from some German comrades, who advise me. I often think of the suggestion you made some time ago as to my travelling, and I should like to be fitted to accept a proposal of that nature should it ever seem likely to serve my purpose. I confess I incline more and more to the idea.

Through all my occupations, my dear Henriette, my heart turns lovingly to you and to my mother in search of that repose it would seek in vain elsewhere. It is a sad fate to have to stifle one's faculty by means of another, because one has no chance of developing them all. God grant I may never be driven to it! Sometimes I am half tempted to try, but the thought of you and of my mother saves me. I shall never really be in my normal condition until I can unite study and meditation with the constant enjoyment of family affection and friendship. My last vacation was perfect in this respect, and is the pattern of what I should desire my future to be. And what air-castles we did build, my poor dear mother and I! You were always an integral factor in every dream. Tell me in your next what your views are as to your own future, and as to returning to France. I have often tried to guess them, but I have nothing satisfactory to go by, and you always avoid the subject with us. Farewell, my dearest Henriette. You know the depth of my affection for you. It is the only return I can make for all you have done for me. I pray I may some day prove my gratitude as you would have me do it. — Your brother and your friend,

E. RENAN.

XIV

MDLLE. RENAN, *Château de Clémensow, Zwierziniec, near Zamosc, Poland.*

PARIS, *February* 13, 1845.

Your last letter, dearest Henriette, pained me exceedingly by its account of the anxiety our long silence had caused you. It was too bad indeed to add that suffering to all you endure for us. Indeed I cannot conceive how we came to neglect writing to you, for our thoughts and conversations were always full of you. You may rely in future on my sparing you a misery of which nobody knows the bitterness better than myself.

I am a little beforehand in writing to-day, because I want to confer seriously with you on the future, concerning which some sort of decision is growing imperative. Up till now I have passively followed the line traced by superior authority, and I cannot as yet find it in my heart to regret having done so. Surely a man too young to act for himself with sense and judgment cannot be blamed if he does not resist a power frequently far wiser than himself, and which is sure to find its own means of enforcing obedience. But the time has come at last when duty drives me to take a personal share in the decision of my future, and play an active part in shaping my own destiny.

The suggestion I have already adverted to of offering me the Hebrew professorship in the Seminary for advanced study, which is to be the outcome next year, so men declare, of Monseigneur Affré's scheme, has taken further shape. The idea that the College would be opened so soon seemed very chimerical to me, and the result has proved me right.

But I have been assured the offer will be ultimately made, though only when my time here has expired. I wonder this was not realised from the first by those who spoke to me of the plan. I assure you it is no disappointment to me. I am rather glad of it, indeed, for I preserve my liberty, and besides, the general characteristics of the proposed establishment do not attract me. There is something belligerent about them, and I have no taste for being a party man. On the other hand, I see the time approaching when I shall be called on to take the irrevocable step connected with the priestly career. Reasonable probabilities supported by wise advice sufficed to guide my preliminary action, but absolute certainty, founded not on external influence and circumstances, but on my own internal convictions, come to of my free and personal will, has now grown indispensable. And where am I to find it?

The silence I have kept upon these painful questions seems to have led you to believe all my irresolution had disappeared. Alas! dear Henriette, my silence was no true type of my busy thoughts. Yet what was the use of harping on a trouble no human power can cure? Through all this painful uncertainty, my one idea has always been, not to decide, to wait — always to wait. Yet I begin to feel waiting is out of season. Supposing I want to retrace my steps when once my own delay has closed every door behind me? So I have had to turn my eyes towards some position which will give me present freedom and future hope, while at the same time it makes the transition easier, and leaves me some way of escape should my sense of duty force me to go back. All my present plans are directed to the conciliation of those two latter objects, and to you, my dearest Henriette, to whom I owe, and gladly shall owe, everything, I turn for help in carrying them out.

My thoughts have reverted to a suggestion you have repeatedly made me, of accepting some position which would couple the advantage of avoiding hurry (as to my ultimate decision) with that of the opportunity of studying life on a wider stage, and often in a truer light, than I can find in books, the only means I have as yet possessed of studying it at all. This course would also serve me to acquire the knowledge without which a man can hardly solve the great problem of life. If the plan is still feasible, I believe this to be the most favourable moment for putting it into execution. I am free from any special engagement, my mind is fairly well cultivated, I have studied closely, and possess a good deal of varied information. I have reached an age at which the first wind is not likely to blow me where it listeth, and yet I have sufficient flexibility of character to realise what is good and beautiful, wherever met, and try to copy it. The accomplishment of such a project would fitly supplement an education still incomplete on certain points, and be a pleasant mode of passing out of my training stage into my actual active life.

Besides the intellectual advantages referred to, it would be the simplest means of inducing the superiors of this house to accept a refusal which may be merely temporary. Prudence would forbid my disobliging them, even if common honesty did not call on me to show them gratitude. And then, too, I naturally desire to relieve those persons who have sacrificed so much to help me as soon as possible.

But as it was you, dear Henriette, who first suggested this idea, you will realise all its advantages as fully as I can. I am quite ignorant as to the nature of the situation you then thought of for me, or how and whether time may have modified your original plan. So I abstain from entering into details. I give you full and free authority to act for me. Everything you have done, so far, has been so good for me, that I cannot do better than place myself unreservedly in your hands. I need hardly tell you that the position which would leave me the greatest leisure for private study, or which would only involve my helping others to learn what would be useful to myself, is the one I should prefer. For my own intellectual progress will ever be my dearest object. The subjects I would rather undertake, and upon which I feel I could impart considerable information, are classical literature and languages, Oriental tongues, science, both mathematical and physical, history (though my studies in that direction are not so deep), and above all philosophy. Indeed, my knowledge of my own facility and my information on various subjects inspires me with the confident hope that I shall shortly be equal to directing another person in any course of study he may select. As to teaching elementary classics, I *could* make up my mind to it if necessary. The locality of my choice would be that in which thought is most advanced, as Germany (the university towns), for instance, and all the more so because I shall soon have a pretty close acquaintance with the language of that country, and that I have been struck by the surprising harmony between my own ideas and the mental standpoint of the chief German philosophers and authors. I leave the whole business, dear Henriette, in your maternal care. I approve beforehand of everything you do, accepting whatever you may settle for me as the work of a beneficent Providence which has always used me well, and chosen you for its active instrument.

Yet it might be wiser, after all, to do nothing decisive as yet. I cannot quite reckon on what the next two or three months may bring forth. Some proposal might be made me here which I could not refuse without an open rupture. If you can give yourself out *as not being certain of my consent*, do what you will. If not, I will undertake to give you a definite answer in a week or two. Uncertain as things are, I still desire to inform you fully of them, so that you may advise me and direct events accordingly. I think the most propitious moment to enter on this new phase of existence would be the opening of next (academic) year. Yet I should not object to spending a good many months of it here. The facilities granted me for attending various courses of lectures at the Sorbonne and the Collège de France, make my stay here useful and very tolerable.

What plans, dearest Henriette! and all for a future I may never see! The thought of death haunts me continually, I know not why. But it does not sadden me, fortunately. I am beginning to face life more resolutely, though doubts still weigh me down. It is so trying to go onward in the dark, one knows not whither. There are moments when I regret man should have been left what little power he has over his own destiny; I would rather it were utterly ruled for him, or else entirely dependent on individual action; whereas now we are strong enough to struggle against our fate, and yet have not sufficient power to direct it, so that the shadow of liberty we possess only serves to bring us misery. Then, again, I console myself by the thought that God orders all things for the best. Farewell, my dear kind Henriette; my hours of trouble are cheered and brightened by your affection. Oh, when shall we be able to tell each other all our thoughts at leisure? You know how sincerely and tenderly I love you.

E. Renan.

Our mother is very well and in good spirits. During the holidays I mentioned the possibility of our new plan to her, and she did not seem averse to it, taking it to be a mere temporary thing. The thought of that beloved mother of ours is very sweet to me, for she is mixed up with all my dreams of happiness. Yet sometimes it breaks my heart to think of her. Great Heaven! what would become of her supposing matters take a certain turn? How cruel it is that the action of a mere youth should produce results of such importance in public estimation. I would sacrifice everything, even my life's happiness, to my mother. Everything save duty! I pray that may not force me to what no other power would make me do. Farewell, beloved Henriette!

XV

February 28, 1845.

I was in the act of writing to you, my beloved Ernest, when your last epistle was put into my hands some hours ago. I put aside the three or four pages I had already written to answer your affectionate letter, every word and every thought in which has sunk deep into my heart. Dear muchloved friend! it is twenty-two years to-day since you first opened your eyes on a world which has been as full of bitterness to you as it has been to me. Since that moment, never an hour has passed in which you have not been my first and tenderest thought. Oh, you are right indeed to turn to me when grief oppresses you! It proves you understand how much I love you; you pay back all I have given you with usury. Yes, my Ernest, before you go further in the career you have entered, before you take another and an irrevocable step in that direction, your mind, as you justly feel, must be absolutely freed from all exterior influence, and your decision must be based on your own personal knowledge, and come to of your own free will. Now, to ensure that freedom, you must escape, for a while at all events, from the atmosphere in which you have lived up to the present; and to acquire the necessary knowledge, it is all-important that you should make some acquaintance with the world in which your life has to be spent; for there are certain things no book in the world can teach you. The idea I suggested is not more difficult nor impossible to realise now than when first I spoke of it, and once I know the plan is to your taste, you may rely, dear brother, on my leaving no stone unturned to carry it out.

Be quite easy as to the secrecy which is so imperatively necessary to prevent anything like responsibility for you, and to avoid compromising your already difficult position. Everything shall be done in my name alone. I will see you are left entirely free; you will not appear in the matter at all. It is I who will have planned and done the whole thing. Further, so as to guard against any possible indiscretion, I will not, in the first instance, anyhow, make use of Monsieur D——, who first mentioned the subject to me. I have other acquaintances whom I can very well ask to oblige me. I will get it done, be sure, but without committing you personally, until I am certain of your approval and consent. Whether I succeed or not, I am firmly convinced you ought to be quite free of your present engagements for the whole of the next twelve months. Do you think the idea of your living independently and studying in

Paris or abroad for a year frightens me? Not at all, my dear Ernest; and if I do not succeed in finding what I want for you, I shall certainly come back to it. Everything I possess is at your service; I can afford even that for you, and I shall be too happy to spend something more, if it brings back a little calm to that poor heart of yours, which I can read even from this lonely spot, and which I know to be so full of suffering and agitation. My heart ached at the thought that Death was in your mind, and that its prospect did not sadden you. Alas! dearest, who would desire to live! if one thought of oneself only? But does such love as mine for you count nothing in your sight? Do you never think, when you dwell with pleasure on such thoughts, of the two women whose dearest hopes and tenderest affections are centred on you? One of your *mothers* indeed you have persuaded of your happiness, but does not *the other*, she who now weeps with you so bitterly, deserve that you should gather up your courage when you think of her? Cheer up, my Ernest, at the thought that you are not alone in the world, that you have a sister, on whom also fate has laid its heavy hand, who is ready to share your sorrows with you, softening them as far as is permitted to her, and who will always find her sweetest consolation in your love. I have played Cassandra's dreary part in all this business of yours. I foresaw and foretold the cruel doubts which now assail you. Nobody would believe me, and I was not strong enough to fight it out alone.

No, dear child, no; public opinion, blind and unjust though it may be, is not so cruel as to attach a responsibility, the thought of which draws such a bitter cry from you, to the action of a youth. I have known several honourable and much-respected men who shrank from the fetters now proposed to you, and nobody has dreamed of making their delicate conscientiousness, too rare, alas! into a crime. What honest man could dare it now-a-days, when those who should only speak the words of peace and goodwill are so often found in the arena of party quarrelling and strife? So do not let that thought dismay you. I do not desire to suggest or advise a rupture, but should you be driven into one by your convictions and your own conscience, fear not that the only people whose opinion is worth a thought will blame you.

Do not let pecuniary difficulties trouble you either. I am prepared to remove them all, at least in so far as my modest means permit me. As to the matter of finding you some other outlook, your brother and I will help you in that too, and we should, I hope, succeed, not perhaps to the full extent of my desire; but after all, my Ernest, would not any position ensuring food and independence, those two prime necessities of existence, be welcome, for a time at all events? Once more I say it, dear brother, I do not desire to incite you to any particular course; I am only anxious — this is indeed my paramount object — that you should have two years' freedom, during which you may judge calmly of the proposal now before you. If after that you desired to take up your old life again, I should not have a word to say, seeing you would do it of your own personal will and knowledge. I cannot think such an arrangement would cost our mother a tear, for I can conceive nothing more precious to her than your repose and peace of mind. Besides, as you have realised already, when a thing becomes a *duty*, every other consideration, however delicate, must bow to its imperious law. When it becomes necessary, we can canvass this tender and most important point more amply.

I do not think it necessary, dear brother, to sum up what I have expressed so fully to you. You realise, I trust, that you have my full support and loving help whatever happens. I flatter myself I foresee every probable difficulty, and should others arise, they would find me ready to face them with fresh courage. So do not be disheartened, my beloved child. Life is full of hard trials. Yours have been early and bitter. But remember you are not left alone to bear them. Whenever you think any indiscretion concerning the steps I am about to take for you less likely to cause trouble, let me know, so that I may ask the help of the person who first advised my inducing you to leave an interval of time between finishing your studies and taking vows. Until you give me leave, I will not mention it to him; I will work through others. But I think that even in his case I could make a preliminary inquiry without compromising you in any way. I will see about it. You understand, of course, that I have several strings to my bow, and that in any case you will have leisure for private study. Ernest, dear child, would I could see you, if only for an hour! I know you are borne down with sadness and anxiety, and I am hundreds of miles away from you. Oh, my God, bestow on him the comfort I am not there to give! Speak words of consolation to his heart, grant him Thy succour and protection!

You will easily conclude from this letter of mine how anxiously I shall wait for news of you. Write to me, then, whenever it is possible, and write, above all, should any fresh sorrow come to darken your soul. I seem to anticipate nothing now but trouble.

I had news of our mother on the very day which brought me your letter of December 1st, and to-day again I have had a letter from each of you. She says she is well, very well indeed, and a line from Emma still further sets my mind at rest as to her health and her surroundings. The previous post had brought me news, too, of our brother and his wife. They, at all events, are happy. May they always remain so! Give our mother news of me. Tell her I kiss her fondly, and that I have her letter, and wait a little before answering it, as she will know I am well through you. It is very late, dear child, and yet I find it hard to say good-bye. Farewell! Be of good courage and trust in those who love you. You cannot be utterly miserable in life while you possess such affection as that I bear you. I have poured my whole existence, my Ernest, into yours. They shall never be parted now, believe me.— Yours ever, and with my whole soul, H. R.

XVI

MDLLE. RENAN, *Château de Clémensow, Zwierziniec, near Zamosc, Poland.*

PARIS, *April* 11, 1845.

How appropriately your last letter arrived, my dear good sister, to comfort my poor heart and raise my hopes. No, indeed, God has not forsaken me while

He spares your faithful generous love to me. So set your mind at rest, dear Henriette, as to the secret suffering and cruel perplexity your heart has guessed in mine. I am too straightforward in my dealings with you to deny my soul has been most severely tried, but your affection, so tenderly and effectually expressed, suffices to temper all its sorrows. And indeed, dear Henriette, I never absolutely lost every gleam of hope, and even in those rare moments when death seemed the only possible solution of all my ills — well, even then there was a certain calm in the recesses of my inmost being. It is at such moments that one feels the blessing of being capable of elevated thought. If happiness were man's sole end, life would be unendurable by those to whom fate grudges it. But when one's affections are set on things above, the tempests of these lower regions toss one less sorely. I drew consolation from the thought that I was suffering for conscience and for virtue's sake. The figure of Jesus in the Gospels, so pure, so noble, so calm, so far beyond the comprehension of his devoutest adorers, was especially supporting to me. When that sublime ideal of suffering and virtue was conjured up before me, I felt my strength return, and I was ready even to suffer again. "My God, if it be possible, let this cup pass from me. Nevertheless not my will, but Thine, be done."

I must begin by telling you, dearest Henriette, that, in accordance with your advice, and with what appeared to me my duty, I have refused to become a subdeacon this year, as was suggested to me. This step, as you are perhaps aware, is looked on as irrevocable. I am convinced my action in the matter will have no disagreeable result. Before beginning to discuss our plans, I should like to complete the picture I have already given you of my present condition of mind, so that you may thereby direct the measures you are good enough to take on my behalf. I do not remember ever having set forth the reasons which have made me cease to incline towards the ecclesiastical career. I should like to do so to-day with all the clearness of a frank and upright nature addressed to an intelligence capable of understanding it. Well, here it is in a nutshell. I do not believe *enough*. While the Catholic faith was the incarnation of all truth to me, its priesthood was invested in my eyes with a brilliant fascination, compact of dignity and beauty. Though some accidental circumstances, merely human, may have somewhat checked the spontaneous impulse of my soul, they were mere clouds, which passed away as soon as I came to understand that every condition of life involves such trials, and some far worse ones. At this very moment I am disposed to scorn them more than ever, and if God were to grant me that divine inspiration which puts its finger on the truth and makes all doubt impossible, from that instant out I would consecrate myself to the service of Catholicism, and would face, not death indeed — for in these days that does not enter the question — but scorn and reproach of every kind to defend a cause which had gained my full conviction of its truth.

But all this time my brain was working desperately. Once roused, my reason demanded its legitimate rights, which every time and every school of thought have granted. Then I fell to verifying Christian truth on rational grounds. God, who sees the secrets of my heart, knows whether I did it faithfully and carefully. Who, indeed, would dare to pass light and trifling judgment on doctrines before which eighteen centuries have knelt? If I had any weakness to contend with, it was that I was favourably rather than hostilely inclined towards them. Had I not everything to make me lean towards being a Christian — my future well-being, long habit, the attractive power of the teaching in which I had been brought up, which had tinged every idea in my existence? But all had to give way when once I saw the truth. God forbid I should say Christianity is false, that word would prove my intelligence very limited. Untruth could never bear so fair a fruit. But it is one thing to say it is not false, and quite another to assert its absolute truth, at least as those who profess to be its interpreters understand it.

I shall always love it and admire it. It has been my childhood's food, my boyhood's joy. It has made me what I am; its moral law (I mean that of the Gospels) will always rule my life. I shall never cease to loathe those sophists (for such do exist) who attack it by calumny and dishonest means. They understand it even less than those who follow it in blind obedience. Above all, Jesus will always be my God. But when from this pure Christianity (which really is reason personified) we come down to the narrow shabby ideas, to all the mythical stories, that fall to pieces at the touch of candid criticism . . . Henriette, forgive me for saying this to you! These thoughts do not express my absolute opinion, but I am full of doubt, and it is not in my power to see things other than as they appear to me. And yet they tell me I must accept the whole thing, that unless I do I am no Catholic! Oh, my God, my God! then what am I to be? Here you see my condition, my poor Henriette. . . . All these speculations are nothing as between you and me. But I want you to understand my position. Yes, I say it again, this is the one bar to my taking orders. Humanly speaking, it would suit me. The life would not be very far removed from that I should lead in any case; it would ensure me a future quite in accordance with my tastes; everything about it would seem to unite in making matters easy to me. I may even say to you that the reputation I have already acquired would end by raising me above the insipid common herd. But duty comes before everything. My mother! that is the one thought that breaks my heart. But there is no help for it.

Let us turn to our plans, dear Henriette. I think you should go forward, but gently, and above all not letting my action appear as anything but a matter of delay in certain quarters. This is really true in fact, and if I had to make a decided retrograde step, I would yet wait awhile. Supposing I did not so wait, and that further reflection brought a revulsion of opinion with it, what should I do? I will never accept your proposal of a year of independent study. God knows the idea in itself is pleasing, but I should be too wretched at the thought of all it would cost you.

No, dearest Henriette, I am very well off here, where I am treated with every kindness. And I can conscientiously stay on, because I only doubt as yet, and if all the doubters were to depart, the place would soon be very empty.

An ordinary tutorship would only suit me in so far as it offered facilities for my own intellectual improvement; for otherwise it would not do me much future service. I have sometimes thought of graduating at the University. A few weeks of study would suffice to ensure my Bachelor's degree. But I have my doubts about the University. Not that I agree with the exaggerated abuse I hear some people shower on it, but I know there is a good deal of inquisitorial interference, and that everything there goes by favour. I do not care to struggle out of one bondage only to submit myself to another. I have lately perceived what may be another opening for me. I go twice a week to M. Quatremère's lectures on Oriental languages at the Collège de France. As he has only four or five pupils, I soon made his acquaintance, helped thereto by an introduction from our chief Hebrew professor at the Seminary, who has scientific relations with him. As he is practically at the head of his own department of study in France, I should hope he might push me in it, if he chose. It is one which I should especially like, as I have made considerable progress in it. But I should not settle on any of these plans without studying them more closely. That would be rendered quite possible, if you succeed in carrying out the project you are now working at for me. All the rest must depend on that. So I just wait, dear Henriette, to hear the result of your efforts. So long as the authorities of this Seminary and my mother remain in ignorance, and that the affair takes the aspect I have already mentioned, that of mere delay and self-examination, we need have no fears. Would I had time to tell you all my thoughts! It makes me miserable to think it takes us a whole month to exchange a single idea! Farewell, my dear good Henriette; on you rest all my hopes of happiness. May I some day be able to repay all you have done for me! The uncertainty of my future saddens me deeply. At all events my deepest tenderness is yours. It is the only return I am absolutely sure of making you.

E. RENAN.

XVII

June 1, 1845.

Nothing can increase the love I bear you, my beloved Ernest. But had that been possible, your last letter would have been the surest means to do it. Yes, my dearest, tell me your full mind on every subject, unfailingly and completely, and be very sure your feelings will not only be understood, but shared, and with the tenderest sympathy. It is a month already since this last precious proof of your confidence reached my hands, and if I have not yet told you all I felt on receiving it, dear boy, it is because I desired to wait for the answer to a letter I had sent to

Vienna, and in which I asked a resident there, who is quite devoted to my service, to assist me in taking certain steps which I detailed to him. I have that answer now, and will shortly refer to it. First of all, dear Ernest, I must tell you that, guided by your last letter, I have decided not to apply to Monsieur des ——. What we look at from the point of view of our hearts and consciences is to him, as to many others, a mere matter of expediency. I found this hard to believe, but I have had to submit to proofs. I could not reckon on his discretion with regard to the people about you; indeed, I am pretty sure he would have spoken to them in the very first instance. I therefore turned my attention to another quarter, and the answer just received announces that prompt steps have been taken, the result of which we have now only to await. Keep your mind easy. You do not appear. Everything has been done in my personal name, and, whatever comes of it, you are in no way bound. The whole thing is being carried on, as such a business, dear Ernest, should be, with the utmost prudence and circumspection.

Now, my dear, let us come back to your letter, and let us consider whether, according to what you tell me, the idea of a tutorship is the best for you. How could I blame you, dear Ernest, because there is a doubt in your mind? Does not my own experience teach me that we have no right to refuse to hearken to what our conscience tells us, what our love of truth inspires? Nay, more; once that voice of conscience speaks, we *cannot* close our ears — we *must* obey its command. So, my poor boy, you may be certain nobody can sympathise in all you confide to me better than I.

I will say nothing as to the source of all your agitation, for I sincerely believe that in such a delicate matter every external influence, even that of a man's nearest and dearest, should vanish and be dumb.

So I take up the question at the point where your mind strikes me as having been at the moment your last letter was written, and I confess I can hardly think, according to that glimpse of it, that you can ever go back to your original views and early tendencies. When certain ideas have been roused, they always leave some trace, and the *very slightest* trace, my Ernest, should suffice to stop you short. This conviction leads me to inquire whether a tutorship, advantageous as it certainly would be at present, would be as much so for your future? I decide nothing; I merely submit the considerations raised by this question, so all-important for us both, to your own judgment. Such a position would have the great advantage of restoring you your liberty of thought and action without shock, disturbance, or rupture, perhaps even without formal explanation, for a time, at all events. It would also give you that opportunity we have so often discussed, of learning and watching life on a wider stage, and perfecting your studies by dint of comparison. But if, as I, dear Ernest, am disposed to think, you are tending towards a different career from that on which some would fain have seen you embark, I fear a tutorship may debar you from entering any other line, while in itself offering only a very limited outlook. You speak of your Oriental studies, of your acquaintance with M. Quatremère, of the possibility of his helping you to some advancement in that direction. Is there no danger, dear Ernest, that if you went far away you might break off relations with the learned professor you mention, and make it impossible to renew the acquaintance? I fear it, I must say, and that reason especially prevents my desire for the success of my present efforts being very keen. The course of independent study I suggested to you, and after which I still hanker, would allow of the continuance, and even of the increase, of this intercourse.

It would, I know, be symptomatic of possible rupture in the eyes of those whose interest is all in favour of keeping their hold on you, and who would be sure to take fright at once. I ask your careful consideration of these two ideas, dear Ernest. They may be summed up thus. A tutorship would never give rise to any suspicion of hesitation on your part, and it would be very easy, after the lapse of two or three years, to prepare every one's mind, even our mother's, for a change which might be more shocking if it were sudden. But, granting the alteration in your ideas to be fairly decided, would not such an occupation, causing you the loss of two or three years, make any other career difficult of attainment? Consider this, my dear, my excellent Ernest, while my friends are looking about them, and let me know all your thoughts and feelings without the slightest reserve. As to the delicacy which prevents your accepting my offer regarding your studying independently, let me argue that the ensuring of your future is my first thought, my dearest wish, the one aim of all my labour. How, then, can the consideration of a trifling outlay affect me, when I remember your whole life depends on it? A steady and hard-working youth can live for a year in Paris on twelve hundred francs. If, to ensure your future, that sum had to be doubled, or even trebled, believe me, dear brother, I should not feel a moment's hesitation; I should be too overjoyed to see the way clear before you. All this, of course, would be *absolutely* between ourselves. Have we not agreed long since to hold all things in common?

Our mother writes me you have decided not to take any step towards irrevocable vows this year. I assure you solemnly this neither surprises nor upsets her. She will easily, with time, be led to take other views for you, and for that purpose your temporary residence abroad would be of special service; yet, dear Ernest, it would not do to turn our backs on any other plan merely on account of this consideration. I cannot believe our mother would take a change of resolution on your part as hardly as you fear. Having always foreseen what has happened, I have repeatedly told her she must expect it, and she has invariably replied that her greatest desire was that you should act in perfect independence. So pray be less uneasy on that head; and besides, dear friend, you must remember this is a matter on which there can be no quibbling. "Duty, sublime word! thou profferest no pleasant thing to man! Thou speakest of sacrifice alone, and yet alone thou teachest him his dignity, his freedom!" Do you recognise Kant in this maxim?

I write on my arrival at Warsaw, where I am again for five or six weeks. The journey, the trouble of settling down, the interruptions of town-life, have all added to my work and delayed my letter, which distresses me much, my Ernest, when I think how you are longing for it. I write amidst constant interruption, for my most longing desire is to send you a word or two of quiet, tender affection. But I do thank you, dear brother, for having hearkened to my voice and that of your own conscience, and refused to take the engagements which were being already pressed upon you. I dare not say more. My letter is very reticent, because I am convinced the privacy of my correspondence is not respected. May God and your own reason inspire you. May your love of what is good and true suggest the counsels I am too far away to give you. Ernest, will the time ever come when there shall be free and unconstrained intercourse between these two hearts of ours, which will understand each other so well, and so delight in their mutual support and enlightenment? What a fair dream! Farewell, my well beloved. Believe you are always in my thoughts. Believe I watch over you with the tenderest anxiety, the most devoted affection. — Yours always, and with all my heart,

HENRIETTE RENAN.

I hope this letter will reach you without delay, as I post it in Warsaw. I shall be here till towards July 10th; so if you write to me in the course of

June or early in July, you must address your letter:—

Mdlle. R.,
Zamoysky Palace,
Warsaw.

Manage, my dear, so that I have your answer before I go back to the country. I will let you know as soon as I have any news about what is being done for us in Germany. If you do not feel certain about my direction after 2nd or 3rd July, use the Warsaw address. If I am gone, my letters will be sent after me; and they must come this way in any case.—Affectionate greetings again, dear Ernest.

XVIII

Mdlle. Renan, *Zamoysky Palace, Warsaw, Poland.*

Paris, *July* 21, 1845.

I thank my God, dear Henriette, for giving me one human being who understands me! Yes, in you alone I find the perfect comprehension of my mental state which guesses the delicate shades I cannot express, and the honest broad-minded appreciation that never seeks to decry intentions which I sincerely believe pure, though many people will interpret them so ill. How little do I care for their opinion, so long as I have the assent of my own conscience, and of those persons whose judgment I value, and while the purity of my motives is ratified by the testimony of one whose moral sense far surpasses that of many who are renowned for their great powers of mind! At all events, I shall have acted as few men in my position have done. I shall have fought boldly against a fate which would seem to be my irrevocable destiny, and to which I have seen many others succumb. Shall I ever be able to rise above it? However that may be, the duty to which I shall have sacrificed my all will console every sorrow that may await me. What a wonderful decree of Providence it is, whereby the sweetest and purest joy is hidden beneath the hardest sacrifices man is called to make! Happy he who has the courage to pay the price!

Your reflections on the alternative courses now before me would occur to any reasonable man in my position, and are all familiar to me. The tutorship in Germany supplies present need perfectly, but does nothing towards the future. The other plan, which would involve my taking a more decided step in the direction of some one or other career, offers many present difficulties, but is more likely to secure my ultimate ends. This is my exact position at the present moment. From it we must draw our practical conclusions. Besides the German tutorship, three principal courses are open to me, about which I must have more positive information before I can decide anything whatever. I have often mentioned my intercourse with M. Quatremère; it has grown closer since the closing weeks of the year when I ended by being his *only* auditor, and I had made up my mind to open the subject of my intentions with him after one of his last lectures, when an unlucky incident came in the way. He published a sudden announcement that he could not conclude the course, and all my plans were thus upset. But I am resolved to make an effort in that direction early next year. It will not be a very rapid road to travel perhaps, but it is a sure and safe one, and the small number of competitors I should find on it would spare me that incessant and selfish rivalry, the scourge of every other career, and so distasteful to the ethical and philosophic mind, which, content with being what it is, has no desire to fight or struggle with the vulgar herd.

A second course, to which I am more inclined, has been suggested by one of my professors, who has certainly given me the impression of being more just and impartial in his views than any of his fellows. He is clear my proper sphere is at the École Normale. Such advice, given at St. Sulpice, and under present circumstances, would seem to prove him pretty liberal-minded. The chief difficulty about taking it evidently lies in the ecclesiastical nature of my past education. But that does not seem to me insuperable. In the first place, I believe the University authorities would make no objections on this score, if I manifested any intention of entering their ranks. Numerous precedents convince me of this fact, and thus a passage in my last letter, the conciseness of which may have rendered it unintelligible, seemed to indicate that my joining the University, and my entrance into its teaching staff, might probably be simultaneous. If that turned out to be impossible, it still remains with me to enter myself, paying the ordinary fees, at one of those preparatory establishments where one is taken as having got through the University courses of Philosophy and Rhetoric in a period of six months. During which time I would prepare for my admission examination. This idea attracts me greatly. For, as I think I have often said before, my intellectual habit, now of long standing, and favoured as it has been by the life I have led, makes study and meditation quite indispensable to me. Man does not live by bread alone, and I believe I could do better without bodily than without mental food. Public teaching would leave me free to satisfy this need, not perhaps so fully and completely as in the case of an independent savant who can study and reflect in absolute independence — such a condition, which would be my dream, is almost unattainable in France now-a-days by anybody who has to barter his brains to earn his bread. But at all events, it would give me the chance of laying out my life after my own tastes, not to mention the fact that the professorial body holds individual liberty in considerable respect.

There are, as you know, three sections in the École Normale, Literature, Mathematical and Physical Science, and Philosophy. I would take up the third, which I know most about, and which has more interest for me than the others. Those who know me well assure me I should rise high. The difficulties of the sudden change, the impossibility of hiding behind any pretext of its being temporary, the anathemas of the clergy, who are certain to denounce me as a heretical schismatic, would not give me pause, except in so far as they would cause sorrow to my mother. That is a consideration before which I feel everything must bow. This seems to me a duty, and even if it struck me as a weakness, I do not know that I should be strong enough to overcome it. But I hope I should find some means of stilling her fears by giving her other hopes. I will sound her on that delicate point during the vacation.

I have mentioned yet a third course, my dearest

Henriette, which might lead to some opening for me. But it is not very clear before me as yet; it lies in the region of possibilities. I have said nothing so far to M. Dupanloup either of my present condition or my future plans, and I can say nothing at present, for he is not in Paris. Well, I believe him to be large-minded enough to take some interest in both. I know several young men, former fellow-students of my own, who have been in the same position as that I am in now, and whom he has helped immensely, either by backing them up in whatever career they embraced, or by opening some door or other before them. He is generous and noble-hearted by nature, and he has a great deal of influence even amongst those whom his party position compels him to oppose. And, you know, the help of the opposite party is often well worth having.

I conclude, then, that I had better not settle anything until I have spoken to him. Yet your proposal, dearest Henriette, is certainly the one that tempts me most. The advantage of keeping everything quiet for the time, at least; the pleasure of visiting Germany, and of completing my views of life by seeing it on a larger stage; the opportunity for knowing men and things, would outweigh every other consideration, even if I did not instinctively incline to follow the impetus given me by your hand, which has always guided me so faithfully.

I have taken no official step as yet within this Seminary. Only three of the chiefs are supposed to be in my confidence, and they are under the impression that I am coming back next year — at the beginning of the academic year, at all events. As for mother and Alain, I have not breathed a word to either of them.

This, then, is the state of things at the present moment, dearest Henriette. Their natural and practical outcome appears to me as follows: I cannot decide anything before the beginning of the next academic year, because I cannot have a quantity of information indispensable to my decision before that date. My idea would be to return here towards the end of the vacation, and then take some decisive action. I would consult M. Quatremère and M. Dupanloup; I would make inquiries about the École Normale; I would settle everything with the heads of this Seminary, for my position obliges me to treat them with great consideration, and thus I hope to have come to some decision by the early days of November. As you may imagine, I shall not be sorry to leave all these plans rather undefined while I am with my mother. I could not conceal a positive resolution from her if I had made one. And I can settle it all with her better from a distance than when we are together.

But a great question, and one I feel very uncertain about, is whether I should re-enter this Seminary or not? Seeing I have decided not to remain in it, the idea of coming back to it seems questionable. I should even feel it to be a matter of conscience, if the heads of the establishment had not strongly pressed me to return, in spite of my straightforward and clear explanation of my ultimate intentions. I know there would be certain advantages in coming back — I should have more facilities for making arrangements with M. Dupanloup and the authorities here, and then it would calm our good mother's feelings.

But truly, why I know not, I shrink from doing it. To come back for a few weeks like that seems to me rather insincere, and even underhand. My vacation experience will help to decide the point. There is a good hotel close to St. Sulpice, about which I have already inquired. I could spend three weeks or a month there very cheaply, and I am sure that time would quite suffice to enable me to make a thoroughly well-considered decision. It is the expense that frightens me, dearest Henriette, and if you are not able to give me an answer about the tutorship in the course of a few months, I could apply to the authorities here, who would receive me with open arms. For when I touched on the point before, they did everything in their power to overcome my scruples about it. Your letter will have great influence as to what I decide.

In two days more, my dear Henriette, I start to join our dear mother. This brings another difficulty which I had to think over long before the right line grew clear. This is the one which recommends itself to me. Almost as soon as I arrive, I will mention our German plan to my mother. I am *certain* she will be pleased with it. I spoke of it vaguely once before, and she seemed much inclined to it. When I told her later that I was learning German, she herself remarked that it would be useful for me when I carried out my plan, and above all, she added, it would bring me nearer you. The poor dear soul fancies that once I am in Germany we must be close to each other. Would to God the idea were something more than the dream of her loving heart. Further, I will let her perceive that many doubts are stirring within me, "that I might, perhaps," &c., &c. In a word, I will set the matter before her as I did some six months since; that is, as an excellent situation for me to occupy while I looked about me before settling down for good. But I shall tell her nothing whatever of our other plans, and indeed I think it very probable the German one will gain the day. In any case, even if it does break down, it will have served her as a stepping-stone to more decisive and disquieting resolutions, which it might be imprudent to put forward at first.

The letter which I expect to receive from you during the vacation will do much to make her take the view I hope for. I entreat you to conform to the idea I have suggested, and which I believe the only practicable one. Write as you would have written six months since. Describe the post as offering a useful means of spending the years during which I cannot come to any irrevocable determination. Do not appear to imagine the possibility, or at all events the existence, of any other hypothesis. Be sure I shall understand all you say. If you think I should not re-enter the Seminary, you will suggest that course, only advising me to go back to Paris towards the close of the vacation, so as to settle it with the authorities. As to the tutorship, you will describe it as it is, but as being very nearly a dead certainty, provided I have patience enough to wait for it.

As regards the École Normale, if you approve that plan, you will advise me to *take my degrees*. I shall know that means to take steps about that business. Thus arranged, the matter could not possibly alarm my mother. O Heavens! what it costs me thus to deceive one from whom I have never hidden anything before! How heavy my subterfuge lies upon my heart! But surely it is my duty to neglect nothing which may soften the heavy blow stern duty forces me to give this best of mothers. Should I not keep silence as far as that is possible? Oh, how willingly I would bear the sorest suffering, if by so doing I could save her a moment's sorrow!

Here, dearest Henriette, you have the rule of conduct I have laid down after much serious thought. Go on as you have begun, on your part. If you find a really advantageous position for me, which will give me some leisure and opportunity for carrying my studies and the course of my intellectual improvement, accept it without any hesitation, sure that whatever you do will have my full approval. If your efforts do not result in anything answering to your wishes for me, act as if you were not quite sure of my consent. But your quick instinct will guide you far better than any words of mine. It is enough for me to make you aware of how I actually stand.

All these matters vex my soul, dear Henriette, and cast it into cruel perplexities. I am calmer, perhaps, than when I was so full of doubt; but the future, which never seemed so close on me before, fills me with anxious fear. Who am I, weak and inexperienced as I am, isolated and unaided, with no one to support me save you, my Henriette, you who are

500 leagues away from me, that I should tear such mighty bonds asunder and break from the path in which superior force has driven me until now? I tremble at the thought. But I will not go back. And then, think you I can part without regret from the beliefs and from the projects which have been my life and happiness for so many years? And all this religious world to which I have grown acclimatised, will it not disown me? And will the outer world again have aught to do with me? In that other one I have been loved and tenderly treated. I still have a kindly feeling for it.

Henriette, dear Henriette, help me to be brave! Oh, how the thought of you supports me when life looks sad and hard, as it does now! For, after all, I should be utterly alone in the world if I had not you. If I were only certain of realising my ideal and being what I long to be! But sure as I may be of myself, who can be sure of circumstances? How often have I cursed the day I first began to think! How I have envied the children and the simple-minded folk I see about me, all so peaceful and happy! May God preserve them from my fate! And yet I thank Him for it!

Farewell, my dear good sister. Teach me to hope for happy days!—Your brother and your friend,

E. RENAN.

(Below.)

I think of returning to Paris towards the 10th of October, or even earlier. I hope for another and more explicit letter from you then, entering into all the questions I have touched on in this. And, if you will, you might send it to Alain, and desire him not to give it me till I pass through St. Malo on my way back. This would obviate any uncertainty about the direction.

(On the margin.)

Your last letter, dearest Henriette, seemed to express a fear that the privacy of our letters had been violated. I can assure you that would be physically impossible without my becoming aware of it, as far at least as the interior of this Seminary is concerned, and I have not said one word to my mother. I fancy I know what has made you imagine this — an unlucky letter I wrote to Trécy, one of my college friends, to whom I could say anything, for he was in very much the same case as myself. A sudden illness carried him off before my letter reached him, and it remained in my mother's possession. Even in that I did not refer to any future plans.

XIX

August 5, 1845.

This very day, dearest friend, the letter for which I have been sighing so wistfully has reached my hands. I was at that moment writing to dear Emma, and take advantage of the fact to beg her to give you these few lines privately. My full answer shall be sent as soon as I can possibly write it. These lines are for you *alone;* do not mention them. Your letter, my Ernest, agitated me much, but it gave me great delight, for I see your resolution is beginning to take shape. I note some signs of the energy and power of will I have so earnestly desired for you, and failing which, we can be nothing but great children to our life's end. Courage! oh courage! my best of brothers! Yes, the law of duty is immutable, and once that speaks, any neglect of its suggestions becomes a crime. Though I am taking precautions to ensure these lines falling under no eyes but yours, I dare not speak quite freely. I will only say your idea of taking your degrees has more than my approbation; it has all my sympathies. It is the plan that attracts me most; it would make my mind easier about you than any other, and there is nothing I am not ready to do to second it. You are right. A man who would give you such advice, holding the position this one holds, must be an honourable man. If there is no insurmountable difficulty in the way, listen to him and follow his wise counsel. Your idea of going back to Paris before the close of the vacation is perfectly sensible and good. But I *insist*, my dear boy, on your taking private lodgings, not only for the time you mention, but for much longer should it prove necessary. Let us have no shilly-shallying or false reckoning about this. I will go into the matter fully in my next letter, but pray understand I consider the point *essential*. You will find more detailed information awaiting you at St. Malo, and you will see I have provided for pressing needs. If the hotel you mention should not suit you, I can easily have board and lodging found you in some respectable house. It might be the better plan. I will have preliminary inquiry made in any case. That will bind you to nothing. But pray do not close with that other proposal. If you should want to write to M. Quatremère, I can find means of sending him your letter. I am personally acquainted with M. Stanislas Julien, who, as you know, holds the Chinese professorship at the Collège de France. I have heard him speak of M. Quatremère as of a person with whom he had frequent intercourse. If it served you in any way, I should not the least mind asking him to be good enough to deliver your letter. . . . But when I think of it, you will be back in Paris before I could get your answer and address my request to him from this distant place. Your own personal action will answer much better, and be more prompt in its effect. Don't neglect moving in this matter, and as soon as you reach Paris, if possible. The sooner the whole thing is cleared up the better, for until then we shall not know what our line should be, and certainty as to that is most important. I only trust the people you will have to do with may be in Paris early in October. I have no news from Germany, but I am sure something is being done. I will let matters there take their course, and we can always decide on what seems best according to the settlement you make.

Do not worry about our mother. Wait till you see the excellent arguments my next letter will contain. If you should have to go further later on, I will undertake to do still more in the same direction. In the letter I shall send you, the words "taking your degrees" will appear to be employed in their ordinary sense, but you will easily decipher the real meaning under my vague expressions.

My St. Malo letter shall be there before the end of September. Ernest, my whole soul longs to be with you. Oh, why are we apart at such a moment?

Courage, dear friend, once more I say it. Bitter struggle is the indispensable condition for attaining true manhood.

Brother! Friend! Beloved child! lean ever on my heart and on my arm, sure that neither will ever fail you. . . . Listen patiently to all that is said to you, but let nothing shake your resolution. Above all, let nothing induce you to swerve from the path your *duty* bids you follow. Let me again repeat, that once certain veils are raised, they never can be dropped again. Farewell now, for a day or two, my dearest one. I am yours unchangingly. Emma will not know why I send you this letter privately; she believes it concerns my own affairs.

This letter is addressed: "For my Ernest. For him ONLY."

I once more confide these lines to my dear Emma, earnestly begging her to remember the request my letter to her contains.

XX

August 15, 1845.

Your last letter so fills my thoughts, beloved friend, that I cannot but reply to it at once. The position in which you, or rather in which *we* are placed — for anything concerning you cannot fail to touch us all

— requires our calmest reflection, and every effort of our reason and conscience must be turned to remedying it. Let us not forget that these two voices represent the voice of God within us. In the first place, I entreat our good mother to join you in weighing the considerations I am about to lay before you in all seriousness, and to forgive me if I dare to speak of advice and experience in her presence. I venture to do so, first of all, because your peace and happiness are my first earthly thought, and also because the vicissitudes of life have doubled in my case that knowledge of events and things and of the human heart which generally comes with years. Oh, may the fruit of my experience and my suffering serve those for whom I would so gladly sacrifice my all! . . .

From the very outset, dear Ernest, I have incessantly warned you of the danger awaiting you on the termination of your studies. I mean the danger of binding yourself blindly and precipitately. Your upright soul must understand this, I felt, and your last letters have proved my hope was not unfounded. For that I thank Heaven deeply. I have always thought, and several years of reflection have only served to strengthen my conviction, that a pause should be made between the end of a man's education and the beginning of his actual life, to give him time to take a calm and unbiassed view of what is to be his permanent undertaking.

Though the course of events, in some cases, renders this wise maxim difficult in practice, to neglect or overrule it appears to me a downright crime, when the career in question is as exceptional as that towards which you have been urged from your youth up. Oh, what a terrible responsibility must lie on the conscience of any family which would press a sacred and indissoluble engagement on a youth not yet capable of realising its nature! This then was my idea when I spoke to you, two years ago, of a tutorship in Germany: to give you time to collect yourself, and to spend that period in a manner that might serve your intellectual development. The idea of suggesting the occupation as your ultimate career never occurred to me. I always looked on it as a temporary measure. You realised that, dear Ernest. You felt your welfare to be ever my first object and my most pressing need. Oh, how I thank you! The Viennese friends, who only needed a word from me to secure their fullest help, are as convinced as I am that their efforts will end by finding what I have suggested to you. It is a mere matter of waiting, for a few months, it may be. The German nobility spend all the summer at their country places, and do not return to town till

P

towards the close of the year. So no inquiries can bring much result till that season and during the months following on it. But this delay, dearest friend, far from being a drawback, will enable you to take certain steps and acquire certain knowledge which appear to me *essential* at this moment, whatever your ulterior views may be.

I have always greatly desired, and I think I have often told you so, to see you in a position to take your University degrees. This is generally regarded as the first step in any career. Whether a man be a layman or an ecclesiastic, an established reputation for knowledge always increases his value in the eyes of those whose judgment is worth anything. The Bachelor's degree is the first step in this direction, and to it I hope you will turn your endeavours as soon as you return to Paris.

I know the nature of the teaching you have had is an obstacle in the way of your at once attending the Sorbonne courses; but I also know, as so do you, that there are possible means of arranging this difficulty, and as a last resort, you can always enter your name at some preparatory establishment. I do not dwell on all this, knowing you to be fully informed. I only desire to urge the necessity of your having your Bachelor's degree, and I beseech you, dear Ernest, to give this your full and prompt attention. No matter if it takes you six months, or even a year, I say again the matter is all-important. The German scheme will *always* remain open to us. I possess the most devoted and valuable friends and acquaintances there, and you will realise what weight your having passed an examination and obtained a diploma would give any recommendation of theirs.

It is indispensable, dear Ernest, in face of these important steps, and on account of the preparatory work and study for these examinations, that you should be quite free; and in my opinion you should not take up your board and lodging in the Seminary on your return. Such a course would fetter you, or, at the very least, it would cause you inconvenience and injury at a moment when you need all your freedom of action. To my mind, the wisest, and indeed the only feasible plan to ensure success in your examination, would be to take a student's lodging and keep quite free of any other occupation.

Another reason, besides that connected with your degree, makes me desire you should follow my advice on this head. You have frequently told me your historical studies are far from complete. It is of the first importance that you should apply yourself to them this year, and follow the great public lectures given in Paris on such subjects as closely as possible. This is a matter of the utmost moment.

History is a thing every one must learn, and now-a-days, when historical research occupies such an important position, full knowledge on that subject is imperatively demanded.

To this end, my dear Ernest, as well as for the preparation for your degree, it is indispensable that you should have full command of your own time, and be able to go and seek any details you may need in our rich public libraries and other great centres of information. Therefore I should like you to move to Paris before the end of the vacation, to come to some understanding with the heads of the Seminary, settle the matter with them, and then turn your attention to the plan I would press on you with all the strength of my affection and all the weight of an experience ripened by events. You know as well as I do that nothing is easier than for a young man to settle in Paris in the manner I describe; but to save you all trouble, I have sent for information as to various details, which I will pass on to you as soon as it reaches me, and which, I hope, will quite satisfy you. As I may not receive it in time for it to reach you at Tréguier, I will send it to Alain, who will give it you as you pass through. Let no mistaken idea of economy check you, my dear Ernest. That would be to misunderstand our *interests* sadly, even taking the word in its purely *material* sense. Try and fit yourself for the *highest* functions, whatever line you may choose to enter upon ultimately, and rest assured that to *be chary of the seed you sow* would not only be a very fatal speculation, but a serious moral blunder. "To whom much is given, from him shall much be required," says the Gospel, and the man who hid his talent was punished as though he had been a spendthrift. How wonderful are the teachings of that book, Ernest! and how many of us fall away from them! Friend, let us try at all events — nay, let us strive our utmost to develop the gifts God has bestowed on you.

You may be sure I shall approve your final resolution, whatever it may be. I will say more: it will give me happiness, once it is the evident outcome of an enlightened mind capable of true discernment. But to see you, at your age, so ignorant of the world, of life, of all books cannot teach, cast into the clutches of the irrevocable — that, my Ernest, would be an anguish that would darken my whole existence! and ever, in the depths of my soul, I should hear a voice crying, "Where is Abel, thy brother?"

Spare me that regret, my beloved! Spare our dear mother, too, by guiding these first steps of yours wisely and prudently. It is impossible, utterly impossible, short of abdicating your own reason, for you to bind yourself, at two-and-twenty, absolutely inexperienced as you are, to a career from which there is no retiring, and long experience in which scarcely suffices to impart the elevation of spirit and soul and thought it so urgently calls for. This fact once admitted, I am convinced the means I point out are the best for turning your period of waiting and reflection to good account. So do not neglect my advice, I entreat you. It is inspired by such true regard, so utterly devoid of any personal consideration, that I cannot think it will be misunderstood, either by yourself, dear Ernest, or by our dear good mother. Oh! would I could be with you, though it were only for a day, or even for one hour. I feel my own strong belief would carry conviction to your minds as well.

As to financial arrangements, everything, dear friend, shall be prepared. Alain will have my first instructions, the rest will be sent you direct to Paris. I have all the necessary information on the subject, and the whole thing is much less alarming than you would imagine. People with orderly and regular habits can live economically anywhere, and in Paris thousands of young men of your age lead the life I suggest should be yours for some time forward without any great expenditure. You know all the courses, both in the Faculty of Literature and in that of Science, are free to all comers. All the great storehouses of human knowledge, all the libraries in Paris, are open to the public every day in the week. You can go there and read and compare and take notes in the most perfect peace and quiet. And here let me remind you, by the way, that the Ste. Geneviève Library is warmed and lighted until ten o'clock at night. Seize all these precious opportunities now you have the chance. The measure I propose to you is purely temporary, I repeat. You alone can decide on your ultimate course. But let us at least employ this transition period, often and necessarily — when one does not desire to compromise one's whole future — a prolonged one, in a useful fashion. I could go on for ever, dear brother, for my whole heart is full of what I say; may you take the same view as I do! I have covered pages in telling you what is easily summed up in these words: *Take your degrees.* And to that end study privately, for some months at all events. It will not be possible to attain it without such study, and on any hypothesis it seems to me an indispensable preliminary step. Dear Ernest, I trust you will not misunderstand me, nor turn a deaf ear to my arguments. I need this belief to soothe the sharp and constant anxiety your position gives me. God guide you! and our beloved mother, too! I hope everything from your uprightness of heart and will.

I never mention our money matters, dear friend, for I do not care to weary you with endless figures. But I will say a few words about them to-day, in the hope that my explanation of our pecuniary position may induce you to follow my advice — that being my first and dominant desire. I assure you, my dear Ernest, that, without any imprudence or inconvenience, I can place a sufficient sum at your disposal to carry out this useful and cherished plan of mine. Our family business must be well advanced. I have sent our brother a remittance which should cover the greater part of the expenses, and he promised to give the matter his special attention during his visit to our dear mother. On the other hand, I have made an arrangement with my pupils' parents which will ensure my not being quite without means when I leave their children. So do not fear to accept my offer, I entreat you. I beg this favour of you with tearful eyes, and with all the eagerness my tenderest affection prompts. Some day, my dear, if God should see fit to spare the life of which you are and ever have been the first object longer than He spares my bodily strength, you shall repay it all, with usury. I hope, yes, I do hope, dear Ernest, I have made you understand the advice I give you is thoroughly wise, prudent, and practical. May your own good sense dictate the rest, and may your love of truth lead you to put it into action. I leave you to write to our good mother, or rather, I carry this long paper talk — the first pages of which I have addressed to you — still further with her, for the two letters are as much your common property as is my deep affection.

Farewell, dear friend! You will readily imagine how anxiously I await news from you. — Yours ever, and with all my heart, H. R.

XXI

September 12, 1845.

At last, my dearest Ernest, I can write to you freely, and tell you fully all the thoughts your last letter has stirred within me! There was not one word of untruth assuredly in what I wrote you last; but it tried me sorely to have to stop short so often, to lay stress on what was not my dominant idea, to talk of irresolution when what you had written me proved there could be no such thing for you in future. So now I hasten, dearest brother, to consider the position as it really is, and to draw the natural conclusions from it — all such as to strengthen the opinion expressed in your last letter.

Two chief points are now settled, I trust. The first — that our mother is at least aware you have *many doubts;* and this I feel sure of, for she mentioned it to Alain, while he was staying with her, and did not seem distressed at the idea. The second — which I *hope* is clear, that it is quite decided you will settle down independently as soon as you get to Paris. Starting on this twofold basis, we will now turn to your future arrangements. As I wrote you word, I have begged one of my friends to look out for a quiet, respectable house in which you might have a room, and perhaps your board as well, for as long as may be necessary. I did this the very day I received your last letter; but I am so terribly out of the way here, that I have not been able to get an answer yet. So take a room at the hotel, my dear boy, as you propose, for a time. As soon as I receive the answer I am expecting I will send it on to Alain, who will know your address before I do, and you will decide as you think best, according to the information it supplies.

Your first act, when you get back to Paris, should be to bring your relations with the Seminary to an end in the most dignified and amicable manner, but utterly and completely. You should then see M. Dupanloup, M. Quatremère, &c., and collect all the information you can get about the École Normale. If M. Quatremère thinks you could make a future by addressing yourself entirely to the study of Oriental languages, I should be inclined to agree with you that such a career has the great advantage of saving you from the crowded competition you will meet everywhere else, and which is all the more trying in proportion to one's own consciousness of real merit. Your views on that point are very correct, dear Ernest; do not lose sight of them, if you should see any opening in that direction — and remember that, in this matter, as in every other, you will always find me ready to do what in me lies to smooth the difficulties of the first few steps. Find out, at the same time, whether you can get into the École Normale. Here, too, you must consider the future, think the whole thing over, weigh it well, and then *decide*, my dearest friend, since I cannot be there to help you do so.

Oh! how this horrible separation weighs on me now! I spend my nights thinking about you. How slowly the days seem to drag on towards that happy one, when at last I shall be able to feel we have left the trying time in which I know you still to be behind us. I can never express, my Ernest, the relief it was to me to learn by your last letter that our uncertainties are coming to an end, that, after all your tossings to and fro between your own reason and the will of others, you have at last come to an absolute and independent resolution. As to the German tutorship, let me entreat you not to think

of it unless every other expedient fails you. I
repeat, I only suggested it as a means of gaining
time for further reflection, for I have always felt
that what has happened must come sooner or later.
But now you *have* reflected, and reflection has borne
fruit, you would not be gaining time; you would
only be losing it, and with it, perhaps, your chance
of entering some other career. And besides, my
dearest, as my great object is to spare you discom-
fort, I do not hesitate to tell you that nothing is
more trying and painful than to live under a roof
and with a family which is not your own, and eat a
stranger's bread. If everything else fails us, we
would go back to that of course; but leave no stone
unturned to prevent the necessity of doing so, and
do not compromise *our* future for the sake of saving
a trifle now. Yes, *our* future it is, dear Ernest, for
I cannot think anything can ever part us in interests
or in heart from this time forward.

And now I come to my usual entreaty as to
money matters. For pity's sake, have no doubt or
misunderstanding on that head. I have commissioned
Alain to give you three hundred francs for your
travelling expenses, and for your first month's board
and lodging. Besides this, I am expecting from day
to day to get a bill for fifteen hundred francs, for
which I have sent to Warsaw. As soon as it reaches

me I shall send it to Paris to a reliable person, who will be under the impression the money belongs to you, and who will pay you over whatever you may want every two or three months, more or less often according as you may desire. From the 1st of October out this fund will be entirely at your service, and on it you may reckon, unless some unforeseen circumstance occurs, to defray your budget for the year. If God grants me life, I shall have provided for the ensuing one before this comes to an end. Be quite easy in your mind. I will see you are not left in difficulties, whatever happens. It has occurred to me, too, that you will want different clothes. I think it would be wiser to get them at St. Malo, and come back to Paris dressed *like other people*. Don't you agree with me?

I have given a hint to Alain, from whom I could not and did not like to conceal the present state of matters completely. I have told him you ought to have two suits of clothes when you get to Paris, one to wear every day, and the other to put on when you go to pay your visits; that your slight experience in that line made me think it better everything should be bought at St. Malo; that I left the choice of the things to your taste; that if you agreed with me (as to getting everything at St. Malo), I begged he would see to it, and charge the expense to me; but that if you should prefer doing your shopping in Paris, he was to add a hundred and fifty or two hundred francs to the money he is to give you from me. Wherever you may choose to get your clothes, let me say, dear boy, that a dark coat over a black vest and trousers strikes me as being the best and most suitable dress you could have. Well, dear Ernest, I think I have foreseen everything. If any detail has escaped me, you must lay it down to my absent-mindedness, and you must use all I possess freely, for what little I have is yours as much as mine. As far as money matters go, be quite easy as to what our brother gives you. It is all set down to my account, and we shall never have but one common purse, you and I. Yes, my poor dear brother, happy days will come for us! They are sure to come, so long as our affection and perfect union are unchanged; and what is happening just at present can only knit them closer. I feel and understand and share all the feelings that oppress your soul. It is a cruel moment, I know well, which brings the final break with all that has filled the dreams and made the happiness of the past. The heart bleeds afterwards for many a day. But it is a trial nobody can escape, once one's eyes are opened and conscience begins to speak. "Revealed truth is a law which human intelligence cannot refuse to accept.

It is not my part to open or shut the door to it at will. It enters the moment its coming is announced, and commands me to submit to its behests." A woman wrote the words I quote. They are not the less true and wise for that. I thank God fervently for having roused the thoughts which have brought you to this decision before it was too late. Ernest, console yourself in your present position by considering what would be the condition of an upright man, bound by irrevocable vows to teach and impose on others things which his reason, and perhaps his conscience even, forbid him to accept. That might have been your unhappy fate! How can I thank Heaven enough for having saved you from it? Be of good courage, then; the path is full of thorns, I know, but as at the outset, so at every step, you will find support in the love and tenderness of your sister, your earliest friend, she whose dearest wish, next to that of seeing you happy, is to keep a foremost place in your affections. Let this thought cheer you too, that up to this you have never disappointed me, and that I feel the future will bring me many fresh hopes and compensations, and help me to forget the tears the past has wrung from me.

I need not beg you, dearest Ernest, to write to me, nor entreat you to send me your address as quickly as you can! Knowing my love for you, you will also understand how utterly you fill my thoughts. Until I receive your Paris address, I will communicate with you through our brother; so be sure you let him know without delay where he is to direct to you. I hope you will write me a few lines from St. Malo. Alas! what a trial this distance that divides us is. Supposing this letter goes astray? I wrote to you twice during last month — once through Emma, who must have given you the little note addressed to yourself, and the other time through our mother. Did you get those letters? I am always uneasy about my correspondence, and I have too good reason to be so.

Reading over my letter, I perceive I have said but little to-day about the École Normale. Do not let that make you think I have changed my mind about it. I should always have a leaning in that direction; but not knowing whether you can get admitted there or not, I do not enlarge further on the subject. But do not lose sight of it. Make up your mind and act accordingly, my dear Ernest. I have every confidence in your good sense and judgment. There will be a great clamour over you, of course, but pray do not let that alarm you. What is it, after all, but empty talk, which will be utterly forgotten before many weeks are out, and short-lived anger, easily despised by one who feels his conscience clear, and knows one faithful, loving heart approves him? Let them rage, dear child, and trust your own good sense and my affection.

I am yours ever, my beloved Ernest, yours with all my heart.

Write to me to the Château de Clémensow, near Zamosc, Poland.

H. RENAN.

Superscription. — For Ernest, not to be given him till he arrives.

XXII

September 16, 1845.

DEAREST FRIEND, — I was not far wrong in my calculations, when I wrote, some four days ago, that I was expecting the immediate arrival of information from Paris as to your board and lodging arrangements. The answer I reckoned on came to-day, and I hasten to send it on, although you may thus get two letters from me by the same post. I applied once more to Mdlle. Ulliac, for she is blessed with unfailing kindness of heart, and her devotion to me knows neither change nor limit. The Monsieur Gasselin so constantly spoken of is the gentleman who has been the bearer of all my letters to you for the last two years. My friend writes me as follows: —

"I have just seen M. Gasselin. He knows a

chemist who lets furnished rooms to young men, provided they are *steady*, for they have to go in and out through his shop. He also knows a quiet restaurant close by. If you wish it, he would mention your brother's name at both these establishments, and he would also call on him personally. M. Gasselin would also undertake to make your brother his quarterly payments, and to render him any friendly office. He is a very worthy man, of vulgar, or rather of neglected, education, but very good-hearted otherwise. It has occurred to me your brother might care to enter some school, such as M. Galleron's, for instance (the successor of M. Hallays-Dabot), as a private boarder. I could ensure his being treated thoroughly well there, both as regards intellectual advantages and creature comforts. A great many young men follow this plan, so as to attend their lectures and keep their terms. I will inquire, in any case, whether M. Galleron would take him as a parlour boarder. Besides this, both you and I know M. and Madame Pataud. You know what worthy people they are, and he would be sure to be well taken care of there. So you see it is easy to arrange for his external comforts, a matter about which he must be very ignorant after the manner in which his youth has been spent. All I tell you should set your mind at rest, dear friend. Pray beg your brother, if his mind is quite made up, to come and see us when he returns. We will go upstairs together to M. Galleron, and everything will soon be arranged. Before then we shall have made all necessary inquiries, and your brother will not have to go into a regular furnished lodging."

So as you see, dear brother, we have a choice of plans. Above all, we have the most absolute kindness and friendliness to fall back on. I force none of this on you. I don't make any obligation of your calling on Mdlle. Ulliac. I only desire to say that in case of any difficulty you have money of *your own* in her keeping, and you will find friends in that house, not wise only, but entirely devoted to your service, information of the most valuable kind, and constant news of your sister to boot. Perhaps the hotel you have already mentioned may please you better for the first few days. I leave that altogether to you, only adding that if, as I do not doubt, your private studies are to be of long duration, some other manner of housing yourself would seem wiser to me. Mdlle. Ulliac and M. Gasselin live in the same house. Here is her address: Mdlle. Ulliac Tremadeure, 40 Boulevard Mont Parnasse. The house is between the Luxembourg Gardens and the Observatory. If you did not like to go and see her you might write her a line, asking her in the most polite manner to beg

M. Gasselin to be good enough to call on you. I am sure he would do so willingly. And I am just as sure that Mdlle. Ulliac would receive you with the utmost kindness. All I ask is, that you should not go to her *dressed differently from other people.*

I now come to another and not less important passage in her letter, dear Ernest, which proves she is a *true friend* to me. I told you I was personally acquainted with M. Stanislas Julien, of the Collège de France. Mdlle. Ulliac knows him even better than I do, and knowing he was a great friend of M. Quatremère's, I was anxious to smooth that part of your path by his means. I therefore begged Mdlle. Ulliac to go and see M. Julien, and to ask him, in my name, to recommend you to M. Quatremère's notice, assuring him you come of a respectable family, with one member of which he is acquainted, and that your present change of front, far from being imputed to you as a crime, should be written down the endeavour of an upright and generous heart. M. Julien and his wife have always expressed and apparently felt a kindly regard for me. I am sure he will do us this kindness, and in as delicate a manner as we could desire. This is Mdlle. Ulliac's answer on the subject: "Before your request as to your brother reached me, I had already thought of mentioning him to M. Julien; so that matter is now settled between us. Students of the Oriental languages are, as you say, few and far between. I may safely promise you M. Julien will take the greatest interest in your brother. And once the great point is decided, I will undertake to interest M. Victor Mauvais, assistant astronomer at the observatory and a former pupil at the seminary, M. Mathieu (M. Arago's brother-in-law), and M. Regnauld, Professor of Physics at the Collège de France, in him as well. Your brother is really hard-working; he takes his studies seriously. The gentlemen I mention will think a great deal of him, and he will make his way in the world. Once his bonds are broken I shall be very glad to see him, and then many things will grow clearer."

So, dear Ernest, in this new world, where you dreaded being so lonely, you will find some voices raised to cheer you on. M. Julien is not only a very learned person, he is a worthy and very kind-hearted man. Let hope rise up in your heart, then, my dear brother. You see that, far or near, your sister strives to watch over you in all things. Would I could give my letters wings, that they might fly to strengthen you and tell you you shall never be forsaken so long as the breath of life is in me! Ernest, do not break my heart! Be guilty of no weakness, no imprudent concession. To me, who know your inmost thought, any such thing would seem a crime. And I cannot think my opinion is utterly valueless in your sight. Recollect this is a matter affecting not only all your future life, but also the whole peace of mine, and the only happiness this world can bring me. I am worn out with anxiety. The only consolation I have is in the sense that you are resolved at last, in the hope you will follow my advice, in the thought that you are about to take a modest student's lodging for six months or a year at all events, and that you will spend that time in taking your Bachelor's degree, attending the great courses of lectures on literature and science, and preparing, in fact, for the examinations for admission to the École Normale. Mdlle. Ulliac, whose opinion is so healthy on most points, is also in favour of this plan. She says, "The idea of joining the École Normale is a very good one. That really constitutes a career." But I tell you again that I should be just as well pleased to see you apply your mind exclusively to Oriental languages, provided the learned professor we have so often referred to sees any outlook for you in that direction. Forgive all this repetition, dear Ernest! You fill my heart and mind and thoughts and all my being. Would I could add persuasion to my words — would that this cry of my inmost soul could reach your bodily ears!

Dear beloved friend, God grant your life may ever know affection as sincere and disinterested as mine! Farewell! I have spent a great part of the night writing all this, and even now I lay down my pen regretfully. I am sending Mdlle. Ulliac, by this same post, the bill for fifteen hundred francs I have already mentioned. I received it yesterday. It is payable at Messrs. Rothschild's on November 10th. If you need the whole sum at once you have only to say so. I am sending it to my friend, because in Paris you can never trust servants, especially in young men's lodgings, their rooms always being left more open and unprotected than those in ordinary houses. Farewell once more, dear Ernest! I hope and believe I have overlooked nothing on my part. May your own good sense and upright conscience do the rest! A thousand fond remembrances, my dear one. H. R.

Do not give Mdlle. Ulliac's address to anybody whatever. It is for your own use only.

You doubtless know Messrs. Hallays-Dabot & Galleron's establishment by name. It is one of the best known in Paris, in the Place de l'Estrapade. M. Pataud, an acquaintance of mine, also has a school for youths in the Rue Neuve Ste. Geneviève, near the Rue des Portes. But there are fewer pupils, and its reputation does not stand so high. This would not matter much to you, as you would not follow the school curriculum. The boarders at both these schools attend the Collège Henri IV.

For Ernest, specially recommended to our brother's best care.

XXIII

TRÉGUIER, *September 22,* 1845.

MY DEAREST SISTER, — Never did man receive a letter breathing deeper tenderness and more generous devotion than that last one of yours. It reached my hands at a moment at once solemn and infinitely touching. At the decisive crisis of my life, in the very arms of my beloved mother, it recalled the existence of the stay God grants me in the person of the sister who so gladly heaps sacrifice on sacrifice to ensure the well-being of those she loves! Even if she had taught me nothing for my future guidance save the immensity of her pure unselfish affection, that surely should largely suffice me, dearest Henriette! Must everything be appraised, in this cold world of ours, by the measure of individual interest; and shall the holiest affections of man's nature be given no higher value than one based on selfish calculation? No, my dear one, the assurance of your love will always be more precious in my eyes, a thousandfold, than all the practical benefits it may confer on me. And even should circumstances forbid my ever profiting by them, shall I not still enjoy the sweetest fruit of your affection in knowing how you love me? I have been spending two months of happiness, intense and unalloyed, with our dear mother. To my delight, I find her quite unchanged. Her health seems fairly good, and she bears the trying loneliness of her life with the greatest courage. She lives on her thoughts of her children. Would you could have shared some of our happy talks! If the thought of the future sometimes instils a bitter drop into our present joy, the same affection always reigns alike in sorrow and in joy, and sweetens both to us. May we ever hold such pleasures, which are always in our grasp, even when we seem to sacrifice them, more dear than many other and less pure delights, which cannot be the common lot in any case, and which, mayhap, will never be bestowed! God knows I never shall desire them, unless the others are assured to us.

And now, dear Henriette, I turn to the discussion of the plans suggested in your last letter. A very serious one it is, and indeed nothing but arguments founded on the most serious reasoning would have any present weight with me. As regards the German situation, I am still in the same mind as that expressed in my last few letters, the sense of which you have caught so perfectly. There can be no question of any permanent career there; it is simply one of temporary employment, which would leave me free to complete my own studies during my residence abroad. It follows, therefore, that any situation which would so absorb my time as to leave but little leisure for comparatively independent study, which would give me no chance of grasping the intellectual movement of the country I might be living in — any merely elementary tutorship, in short — would appear very unlikely to suit, unless, indeed, it carried with it those compensating advantages, as to which I have invested you with the fullest powers. But for my part I can hardly conceive the existence of such compensations. Further, it would appear to me, according to the ideas about Germany I have been able to form so far, that Austria is far from being the country most likely to answer my purpose. I do nothing, dear Henriette, but repeat what I have so often said before, and you will perhaps think me terribly hard to please. But the principles expressed in your last letter, which I completely share, convince me we shall agree in our ultimate deductions. Even from the lowest point of view, would it not be mistaken economy to sacrifice years which may be the most fruitful of my life to mere pecuniary advantage? Besides, my intellectual conscience shudders at the thought; I should feel such an act to be a crime. Wherefore, dearest sister, if you can pitch upon a situation offering all the conditions already named you may accept it for me, sure of our mother's approval and my own. But I confess I feel it unlikely such a concatenation will be found, and that makes me look on my journey as still problematical in the extreme.

The case is different as to the idea of my employing the year now coming on in taking my degrees at the university. I have been thinking it over for some time, and our mother spoke of it herself, before you mentioned it in your letters. The matter is quite settled; the only difficulty likely to arise is as to the manner of its execution. The one you suggest, dear Henriette, that of my settling in Paris as a private student, while it proves the greatness of your generosity to me, offers certain drawbacks, at which our mother immediately took fright, and which, I must admit, are somewhat serious. I shall, therefore, not attempt it, except as a last resource, and after every other plan has failed. What are these other plans of yours? I hear you ask. I cannot positively say, my dearest sister — I shall have no precise information till I have been a while in Paris and talked the matter over with all my friends. But the following ideas strike me as feasible. To stop on at St. Sulpice —

the simplest of all, but much the least profitable. I should not find it easy, there, to get through all the work and attend all the lectures necessary for the attainment of our end. Even if the heads of the house were to excuse me from all theological study, which is very unlikely, the general system of the life there is far from being favourable to the carrying out of such a scheme.

M. Dupanloup is more likely to help me to a position compatible with my object. He is certain to offer me something in his institution as soon as I broach the subject, for his staff is far short of its full number this year. But I should be loath to accept any such position, for, as you will doubtless feel, it would make the ultimate execution of our plan well-nigh impossible. The utmost I should care to do would be to undertake to teach history or mathematics three or four times a week. In the first case, the time actually given to instructing my class would be all I should lose; and in the second, the necessary study would be profitable to myself. As to the other duties — such as keeping order, &c. — generally expected of the teaching staff, I should bargain to be completely relieved of them. I would rather, in fact, take rank as a *pupil who helped the teaching staff*, than as an actual instructor. I know several cases which make me believe this ambiguous position possible.

Only last year several youths, both Paris and country bred, resided in M. Dupanloup's college under similar conditions, and with an object absolutely identical to mine. They formed the nucleus of the institution Monseigneur Affré was to have founded for this special purpose, and proposals with regard to which were repeatedly made to me. But that plan is nothing but a plan as yet — and Monseigneur Affré makes more than he can carry out. Nevertheless, taking everything together, I do see a possibility of realising our desire, though I cannot specifically indicate how at this moment. I have other plans as well, but I want to have some certainty of their feasibility before I detail them to you. This I hope to possess within a few weeks, and then I shall lose no time in laying them before you. Rest assured, dear sister, that none but the most serious and conscientious feeling will direct my steps, for which your guidance would be so invaluable. I shall guess what you would say instinctively, and act accordingly.

Though even now I am preparing, as far as local circumstance permits, to take my university degrees, the object of my special holiday study is to increase my knowledge of German literature. As its actual literal interpretation grows less difficult to me, I am beginning to appreciate its spirit, and this initiation marks an epoch in my mental being. I felt as if I had entered some temple when first I gained the power of realising its purity, its nobility, its morality, its religiousness, if I may take that word and use it in its very highest sense. How noble is the German conception of man, and of man's life. How far removed from the paltry standpoint which reduces human aims to the mean proportions of mere pleasure or personal benefit. To me it typifies the inevitable reaction of the human mind against the spirit of the eighteenth century, replacing the too realistic thought and material positivism of that period by the purest and most ideal morality.

That same reaction, as it has taken place here in the person of M. Cousin, and under the form of eclecticism, is as colourless as imitations are generally apt to be. And what a difference, too, in the purity of the moral concept. It reminds one of the difference between Jesus Christ and Socrates! The French school, scared no doubt by the dryness and severity of French Catholic orthodoxy, has kept itself too much apart from Christianity. Every philosopher desires latitude; and Christianity, as it exists in Northern Germany, gives all any one can demand in that respect. German philosophy is impregnated with Christian morality, with its general spirit of love, of gentleness, of chaste and unselfish contemplation, at all events. Ah! who would not be a Christian, of that kind! Especially do I rejoice to find the Germans condemn those systems of philosophy which would fain forbid man to accept the idea of the infinite, and would have the coarsest realism rule in literature, art, and even morals.

Truly life would not be worth living if man's sole faculties were his external ones! Another thing which delights me about these Germans is their happy way of combining poetry, learning, and philosophy. Such a union constitutes the ideal thinker, to my mind. I find the highest realisation of this diverse mode of thought in Herder and Goethe, and they consequently attract me most of all. Yet Goethe somewhat lacks morality. Faust is admirable, as far as the philosophy goes, but its scepticism is heart-breaking. The world is not like that in reality. Absolute truth and goodness do exist. We must *believe* the first, and practise the second. The thought of any different world is a perfect nightmare, and truly Faust is nothing but a nightmare! But what a picture of the anguish of the doubter! As I read some passages, I think I hear him telling my own private history! Never do I peruse the splendid soliloquy, "Wherefore, celestial sounds," &c., especially that fine line, "*Das Wunder ist des Glaubens liebstes Kind,*" without profound emotion. This indoctrination into a new process of thought has helped me greatly in the trying times I have lately gone through. What would become of one, at certain periods in one's life, if study and intellectual culture did not carry one out of the external difficulties with which one's wearied soul is struggling! Though indeed, my dearest sister, all I need to help me bear mine, is the certainty that your heart understands and shares them. God grant me to prove, some of these days, you have not wasted your affection on ungrateful soil.—Your brother and your friend,

E. RENAN.

(Separate enclosure.)

These lines are for your eye only, dearest sister.

Our mother has doubtless seen the rest of my letter. You will know what modification it may require. She was very much averse to the German plan at first; now she is beginning to get reconciled to it. The idea of my studying in Paris alarmed her even more, but I have contrived to reassure her a little. Anyhow, I let her think it unlikely at present, and only a possible and last resource. I have purposely exaggerated all its difficulties, and painted the other plans in rather gay colours. O heavens, my sister, what I suffer! I write this in secret, and almost in the dark. I hoped to snatch an easier chance of doing it, but none has offered. Shall I even be able to slip it into the envelope? I shall have to go to St. Sulpice. Once there I shall follow the course indicated in my last Paris letter. Difficulties bristle all round me, and even worse than I foresaw — I mean as regards our mother. The idea of any sudden secularisation is not to be dreamt of. I have hit on a means of getting the private-study plan accepted. I will get my director, in whom she has great confidence (instilled by me), to write to her on the subject. I did the same at Issy when I was in a difficulty there.

I hope much from the details you will get from St. Malo. Inquire, too, as in your last you said you would, about an hotel or boarding-house. The information will be of great service to me. O my God, into what a net hast Thou led me! The only issue I can see is through my poor mother's heart! I try to cheer her; I have had to soften matters so as to save her pain. And then the struggle in my own mind! Cannot you fancy I have often been on the point of turning back? I can add no more. She is sitting close beside me. God knows I love and respect her from the bottom of my soul. Never was filial affection deeper, and it brings me nothing but pain! Farewell, dear one.

E. RENAN.

XXIV

October 10, 1845.

Our mother's letter and yours both came by the last post, dear Ernest. Your little enclosure claimed all my attention, as you may fancy, for I felt the rest of the letter did not fully express your thoughts. How I have suffered, too, from the signs of failing resolution it bore, compared with your previous ones — from the idea that your strength was giving way in face of the first difficulties confronting you! I pray, with all the strength of my affection, the two letters I have sent you to St. Malo have reached your hands. May they restore your courage! Above all, may they help you to avoid fresh mistakes! I do not reproach you, my poor child, for I see how pitiable your condition is; but let me entreat you not to give way to suffering, and to try and gather strength to put an end to a state of matters which must be perfect torture to you.

You seem to me on the brink of taking up one of those hybrid positions which are nothing in themselves, which lead to nothing, and which, after absorbing one or two of the most precious years of your life, will leave us in the same difficulty as that with which we are now struggling. What, dear boy, must the result be? True, you will have acquired a still greater conviction of the utter impossibility of continuing in the path into which you have been forced. But you will also have made every other line more difficult, by wasting time, or even by employing it, without any settled object. And besides, who knows whether fate may not have some fresh trial in store for me? Will it permit me, *then*, to do that which I shall so gladly do for you at present?

Well, my Ernest, far be it from me to try to force either my view of things, or my opinion as to your proper course, upon you. My sole desire is to beseech you to beware of weakness, which frequently is fatal even to the very persons for whose sake one has been guilty of it.

In the endeavour to spare them unreasonable, and therefore short-lived, pain one may be laying up real and bitter sorrow for them. I cannot understand what could be so exceedingly distressing to our mother in the very idea of your striking out a new line, when it is so evidently demonstrated that your former one cannot suit you in future. Rest assured, my dear boy, that though my love and respect for our mother are as deep as they can be, I should not have hesitated, in my own case, to write to her directly, without any intermediary whatever — "I can go no further, because I lack something which nobody can give me. No human being can *make himself believe.*" That sums up all you have said to me, and it required no effort on my part to understand that henceforth the fetters proffered you could only bring you misery. But I still hope my two last letters may have raised your courage, and stopped you on the dangerous brink of compromise.

In my second I enclosed the information sent me by my good friend Mdlle. Ulliac with regard to schools and lodgings. My one fear is, that this letter may have missed you at St. Malo, and in any case, I am asking Mdlle. Ulliac to get M. Gasselin to repeat what she had charged me to tell you. From her you will gather that you need fear no difficulty in that respect. Mdlle. Ulliac's kind-hearted emissary has, I fancy, found just what you want, and whenever you need his presence, a line to my friend will always bring her neighbour to your side. I gave you Mdlle. Ulliac's address in my last letter. I only trust it may have reached you! . . .

I am constantly with you in heart and thought. I am in a state of the most cruel uncertainty, and by a curious combination of circumstances this condition must last for a very long time. The journey to Italy, of which I dropped a hint to our mother, is now a settled affair. We are to start in about ten days or a fortnight; and in spite of the anxiety with which I expect news of you, I shall have to do without that consolation for many a day. Do not write here, dear Ernest, after this reaches you. But if you have done so already, make your mind easy. The letter will be sent on to me at Vienna, where we are to stay two or three weeks.

If anything is settled early in November write to Vienna, enclosing your letter in an envelope directed:—

>   *Madame Catry,*
>   *Princess Lichtenstein,*
>   *Hôtel Razumowsky,*
>   *Landstrasse,*
>   *Vienna, Austria.*

This friend of mine, who is duly warned, will safely make over anything she receives to me. The inside envelope should merely bear the words, Mdlle. Renan. Let me remind you that Austrian letters must be prepaid right up to the frontier, otherwise they are not delivered. You can direct thus up till the 15th of November, reckoning a week for the transit of a letter. If I get news of you, or if I have anything to tell you, I will write from Vienna.

Not, my dear Ernest, that I desire just now to stimulate the zeal of the persons I have begged to act for you. A tutorship of any kind can only be a transitory thing, and a definite position is now the *essential* matter in my eyes. I understood at once, my poor dear boy, that Austria would not suit you, and I had requested my friends to make inquiries at Munich, not having any hope of getting it done in North Germany, where, unluckily, I have no acquaintances. I say unluckily, and yet I do not greatly regret it, for I can see no advantage, situated as you are at present, in your accepting a position which gives you no future outlook.

Dearest friend, let me say it again, think, pray think of making a career, a future for yourself, and shrink from no sacrifice to attain that end. It was with that view that the École Normale, or the private study of Oriental languages, tempted me for you, and it would cost me much to relinquish the idea. My mind is so taken up with you, dear Ernest, that I can hardly give a thought to the immense journey on which I am about to start. Oh, what a consolation it would be to my poor heart if I could hear from you before I go, and if your letter told me you had decided at last according to my hope and my desire. You may be quite sure you will never be able to go back to your past life; therefore you must apply your mind rationally to making the best of your present position. Your last letter distressed me greatly, but I still hope much from your common-sense, your reason, and your uprightness. You will realise from these incoherent lines that a thousand duties and preoccupations are on me as I write. But through them all I carry one fixed idea—you, my Ernest, always you.

I fancy you will not have been to Mdlle. Ulliac, as I begged you not to go unless you had broken your bonds; and your last letter tells me that is not yet the case. You have never mentioned, dearest Ernest, a few confidential lines which I sent you through Emma. I wonder whether they reached you or not? Pray tell me always what letters of mine you have received in the intervals between your answers. What a torment it is to be in a constant state of anxiety about one's correspondence!

Farewell, dear friend, I have no time to finish this, and it must go to-morrow.—I am yours, my Ernest, yours always, with my whole soul.

H. R.

Please send enclosed note to our mother. I scarce know what I write. I have not even time to read my letter over.

XXV

MDLLE. RENAN, *Château de Clémensow, near Zamosc, Poland.*

RUE DU POT-DE-FER, PARIS,
October 13, 1845.

At last, my dear, kind sister, I can speak unreservedly, and pour out all the anguish of my soul to you. The last few days are marked ones in my life. They may or may not have been the most decisive of my existence; they have certainly been the most agonising I can ever know. So many serious events have been crowded into their short space, that I can do no more on this occasion than relate them. Even that will be a great relief to me, for I am terribly desolate now, and it is inexpressibly sweet to this tired, lonely heart of mine to lean on yours.

One word more, beloved friend, about the vacation, which brought me so much happiness and so much pain at once. My position during it was of the strangest. It is such a joy to me to be with my dear mother, to take care of her, to kiss her, to cheer her with my fancies, that I believe she would make me forget the most galling present suffering and anxiety. And then the fact of being in the country of my birth always gives me an indefinable sense of happiness. All my childhood comes back to me, so simple, so pure, so free from care, and the thought of the old days is full of charm and tenderness to me. Life in that country is commonplace in a sense, but it has a certain repose and comfort about it, especially and most pleasantly favourable to thought and sentiment. Ah! how deeply I feel its sweetness now! I am weak, dearest Henriette. Sometimes I am half tempted to be satisfied with a simple, even common, life; I would make it noble by the dignity of its private qualities. But then I think of you, and I take courage!

Yet even in the midst of so peaceful and pleasant an existence you will easily realise how painful my position as regarded our mother must have been. She had a dim suspicion of my state of mind, and she kept trying to read the meaning of every word I spoke and everything I did. I dreaded her learning the truth, and yet I felt she ought to know it. Conceive my anguish! The absolute necessity of making her understand the actual state of the case, combined with the fear of causing her pain, misled me into doing the most contradictory things, and that faculty our good mother has of interpreting everything in the sense she most desires drove me well-nigh distracted. She would take no hint of any kind. At last one day the hour came (I shall never forget it) when I was forced to speak more clearly. I said outright that I was in a state of doubt, and that I must *wait*. Well, she has been quieter ever since. The journey to Germany, which has been our chief topic, even the idea of my following a course of private study, no longer causes her the same terrors. I have contrived to connect them in her mind with her most cherished plans, with the idea of our ultimate reunion, with the advancement of my studies, &c.

In fact, my dearest Henriette, I am very well pleased with the alteration in her way of looking at things, and I believe that by dint of immense precaution we may be able to save her unendurable suffering. When you write to her, keep two things before your mind. First, that she still believes me to be *undecided;* second, that the course of private study is to lead up to the journey to Germany, which in itself is a method of passing a certain amount of time — a temporary measure, in fact. Do not even let her know, till further orders, that I am at an hotel. Ah, dearest sister, how dear our mother is to me! There lies my greatest happiness and my sorest pain. I should be disgusted to notice signs of triviality in any department of my innermost feelings. I can discover none, at all events, in this particular.

The journey to St. Malo was my first break with the

past, dear Henriette. I found your letters there, and they were a great support to me, as you may think, dear sister; for I had faltered very often, and I do not blush to own it — I believe I faltered for reasons which deserve respect. I told Alain everything, and with his usual admirable good sense he realised and grasped it all at once. He quite agrees with you and me as to the nature of our plans, and the method to employ for carrying them through. His deep and true affection, his acuteness and his upright feeling, have been the greatest help to me. Fanny, too, has been very kind. But I have fought shy of the offers of pecuniary assistance our good brother has not failed to make me, so as to relieve you of some of the burden. Can you forgive this, Henriette? I remembered you had told me you and I were one. Yes, dearest, and one day I hope to have the joy of telling you the same.

I got to Paris on October 9th in the evening. Since that time, dearest Henriette, event has followed on event with startling swiftness. Though firm in my resolve, and well aware that this rapidity served but to hasten its execution, I would sometimes have gladly checked its hurrying speed. As my last letter will have explained, I was obliged, in pursuance of the cautious line I had marked out, to go to St. Sulpice when I first arrived in Paris. I will frankly own that

I believed myself committed to half-measures for a considerable time, and I little thought an unforeseen event would hasten my somewhat lagging feet in spite of me. On my arrival at St. Sulpice, then, I was informed I no longer belonged to that seminary, having been selected by Monseigneur Affré, with several others, to form the institution mentioned in my last letter, and which, so it appears, is to open its doors forthwith. At the same time, I was ordered to call on him in the course of the day and give my answer. You may imagine my state of mind. It grew worse a few hours later when I was told the Archbishop was in the seminary and wished to see me. My conscience imperiously commanded me to refuse to join him, yet it was impossible to give my real reasons, which would have been but ill received coming from a person of whose character he possessed no previous knowledge.

Such, at least, was the opinion of the persons I consulted, and who were good enough to undertake to mediate for me with the Archbishop. The storm blew over, and His Grace was even kind enough to send me a few words of encouragement and hope.

After taking a public step of so clear and downright a nature, I thought it better to lose no time in straightforwardly pursuing the course circumstances had so successfully opened to me, and that very day

I informed the directors I did not intend to spend this year at the seminary. That evening I was in my hotel. All those bonds broken in a few hours, dear sister. Think of it! I have no regrets. I revel, on the contrary, in the supreme calm that comes after the sacrifice, for a sacrifice it was to me. Everything looked so smooth before me, our mother would have been so pleased, and I so peaceful — and then at certain moments my past life would take hold of me again, my doubts seemed to fly away, and my act was evil in my eyes. Yet I felt that was only the momentary result of my normal and intellectual weariness, and I knew whenever I was quietly settled in my own room all my critical faculties would be sure to reawaken. In the course of the next few days I closed my relations with the authorities of St. Sulpice in all dignity and seriousness. The esteem and affection they showed me gave me real delight. I could not have believed such breadth of mind existed here in the very centre, so to speak, of the strictest orthodoxy. They are quite persuaded I shall go back to them. My Henriette, will you credit it? I too like to fancy it, and it was a pleasure to me to hear them say it. Tax me with weakness if you will. I am not a man to espouse a prejudice and resolve never to relinquish it, whatever the scientific conclusions I may ultimately reach; and after all, Christianity is so constituted that I can very well admit a man might judge it differently according to the various phases of his intellectual progress. But at this present moment I see no prospect of any change in my opinions, none, at all events, complete enough to drive me back into Catholic and ecclesiastical orthodoxy.

Once free of my fetters, I had to turn my thoughts and efforts in the direction of some other career. That, in fact, is my constant occupation now, both physical and mental. Things go on steadily, every hour bringing some fresh event, which tends towards the ultimate solution, but nothing is yet absolutely settled. Yet I can perceive near possibilities of the most cheering nature. To continue my journal:—

The morning after my departure from the seminary I wrote to M. Dupanloup and to Mdlle. Ulliac. As I had no lay garments to put on, I could not wait on her in person. I begged her to ask M. Gasselin to call on me. She replied the very next day with the kindest and most obliging letter. It might have been from your own self. Oh, how she speaks of you, my Henriette! How she does love you! M. Gasselin spoke in the same strain. What a delight it is to me to feel we are not the only people who appreciate you! The simple, pure, and elevated tone of all your little notes touches me and gives me strength. On Monday, the 13th, M. Gasselin came to see me. He is acting as my intermediary in the matter of buying my layman's outfit.

I have no answer, so far, from M. Dupanloup. He is such a busy man, it is well-nigh impossible to get speech of him. I called on him, but with no better success. A proposal which I mean to follow up has reached me from the Superior of the seminary. He desires to get me into the Collège Stanislas in some capacity or other, and promises me every sort of recommendation to the Principal, M. Gratry, who is his intimate personal friend. You will understand I cannot well accept anything which would involve too heavy duties, or which did not leave me very many hours for my own work. But I will do my best. The Professor of Hebrew and Scripture at the seminary has also promised to recommend me at once and very strongly to M. Quatremère, whom he often sees. He has a great feeling about me, as I am his favourite pupil. I have often acted in scientific matters between him and the learned Professor of the Collège de France. To wind up, dear Henriette, unless I am mistaken, we have two questions before us, each quite distinct from the other. Firstly, "Where am I to settle down. In the Collège Stanislas, the Pension Galleron, &c.?" And secondly, "To what branch of study shall I ultimately devote myself.

Shall it be the École Normale or Oriental languages?" The solution of the second question must clearly wait till after the first is settled, for it demands a world of information not to be collected in a day. I cannot go to Mdlle. Ulliac and talk it all over with her personally until I have proper clothes to wear. That must surely be in the course of two or three days, and I am confident I shall not have to spend more than a week in all at an hotel. The one I am in now is really not dear, and very decently comfortable.[1]

I must tell you, dear sister, that I am absolutely resolved not to live the whole of this year at your sole expense, and I have quite made up my mind to accept some temporary post which will not take up much of my time, and which will, to a certain extent, be useful to me. Something Mdlle. Ulliac dropped has made me think this possible. On the whole, dear friend, I am fairly satisfied with the way in which things are working out, and I have little anxiety on that score. But what external benefits can ever compensate for the suffering I am obliged to inflict on our beloved mother, and the heartache the severance from my happy past has cost me? Ah, how many springs of happiness must be dry to

[1] The hotel kept by Mdlle. Céleste, and mentioned in the "Souvenirs de l'Enfance et de Jeunesse."

me henceforward! And never, never can I drink of any that yield coarse or vulgar pleasures! Here ends my journal, dearest, up to this 13th of October. If I were to send it off at once I might perhaps have to write again to-morrow, for to-morrow may decide my fate. But then, again, I might be tempted, by this consideration, to put off sending it from day to day until it is too late. It is long, too, since you can have heard from me, and my last letter was not over satisfactory as I remember. Till to-morrow then I keep this back, but to-morrow without fail it goes.

Wednesday, 15th October.

All this business makes my head swim. I am perpetually thinking I see the end of it, and then it all begins again. Yesterday I was convinced everything would be settled to-day, and I put off sending you this letter. To-day I believe all will be arranged to-morrow, but I am resolved you shall not suffer any longer by my silence. We are really getting on. I have seen M. Dupanloup, and was delighted with him. He granted me an interview which lasted an hour and a half, a perfect miracle for him. Oh, how he understood me! Oh, how he helped me! He brought me back to that higher sphere of thought from which my sharp anxieties and the conventionality of the people with whom I have had to deal had somewhat dragged me down. I was quite frank and explicit, and he was very much pleased with me for being so. I recognised the man's superior qualities by the clear and straightforward line of action he recommended. He has promised to do *all he can for me*. I have also seen M. Galleron. He does not take private boarders, but he has recommended me to a friend of his who keeps a school (M. Crouzet, Rue des Deux Églises, you must know the school), who has offered me a position in his establishment which would ensure me board, lodging, and laundry expenses, while the duties to be fulfilled in return are very fair and reasonable.[1]

Then I have seen the Principal of the Collège Stanislas and several of the directors. I brought recommendations with me, and found several old acquaintances as well who spoke for me. I must confess the college tempts me; I feel, dear sister, I should be fairly and honourably treated there. You may have some fears indeed, for a certain proportion of the staff are churchmen, but the constitution of the house is purely academic. And I have been exceedingly plain-spoken with the Principal as to the reason of my leaving the seminary. See what a capital mode of transition thus offers! Nobody will wonder

[1] The present Rue de l'Abbé de l'Épée.

at my going from St. Sulpice to the Collège Stanislas, and not a soul will be surprised at my moving on from the Collège Stanislas to some other house connected with the university. And my mother will be delighted. She has mentioned the college herself, and pressed me strongly to enter it. I go no further into the subject just at present. I await the communications promised me by Mdlle. Ulliac and M. Dupanloup. I can do nothing till I get them. But I must confess I desire and hope for a successful conclusion. Forgive the horrible confusion you must perceive in my ideas, dear sister. All these practical matters weigh me down and harass me. I have sworn allegiance to an order of things far superior to such petty questions, and I will cling to it in spite of every hindrance. What would life be if it were all made up of such trivialities!

Farewell, my dear, good Henriette! When I think of you, and read your letters over, and recollect that you, a woman, have suffered so much more than I, I take fresh courage. Write to me soon, through Alain, through Mdlle. Ulliac, I care not how. I hope you will have another letter within a day or two—by this very post, perhaps—announcing some definite conclusion. Till then farewell, my sister. You know how tenderly I love you.

E. RENAN.

Do not write to our mother till you have got my next letter; or if you do write, let her think I am still at St. Sulpice. Leave the next few moves as regards that delicate point to me. I will let you know when it is time for you to take the initiative in my place.

XXVI

Paris, *October* 17, 1845.

At last, my dear sister, I can give you a definite reply. All that called for decision, and was capable of it, just at present, has been settled. Only those ulterior questions remain which need leisurely discussion after closer examination of our circumstances. Let me hasten to tell you, anyhow, I am not bound by any engagement, and by to-morrow morning what is done can easily be undone.

It is at the Collège Stanislas, dear sister, that I propose to sojourn for the next year. Let me pray you, in Heaven's name, not to start back at a name which, so I am told, may be displeasing to you! Hear me out. I have accepted a post as usher. I know how ill that sounds, and all the discomforts the position involves; but I must put a good face on it, and not expect to find my path bestrewn with flowers at the very outset. Well-informed people assure me that, in spite of my duties, I shall have all the spare time I could desire. I shall have six hours of perfect freedom every day. As the classes are small, too, and the one I shall have to look after consists of the most advanced pupils, I shall be able to go on with my work even during school-time. And I have acquired a certain amount of habit of working in surrounding disturbance and even downright noise. I am to receive six hundred francs a year, food, firing, &c. This, dear Henriette, is the post I have accepted. Now let me enumerate the reasons which inclined me to doing so. Then I will add those which made it both a *duty* and a *necessity*.

In the first place, dear sister, I shall find within the college all the necessary facilities for taking my degree. *Special* courses for preparation, given for the benefit of the teaching staff, who are still *students*, and a special library for the same purpose. One of these courses is delivered by the Principal, another by M. Lenormant, another by M. Ozanam. The two last named are professors at the Sorbonne. Thus I shall be in contact with distinguished and influential men, whose advice may guide me through this university career, which is more complicated than you would think; and I shall be fairly and honourably treated. The religious and semi-ecclesiastical character of the institution is a sure pledge of this, and my first relations with its chiefs have proved it. You must admit that amongst Christians and ecclesiastics worthy of any respect one meets with an amount of kindness, of charity, as they themselves call it, not to be found elsewhere. This contrast has struck me sharply of late, since I have had to do with the two different classes of people. For instance, your schoolmasters have struck me as being disgustingly hard and fast in their ideas. I believe they simply desired to use me as a tool for successful speculations. Never! my dear Henriette, never! I must be conscious of a sense of morality within me and around me too. And further, dear sister, a college is a centre where favourable opportunities occur more frequently than elsewhere, because life there is more full and active. I am supposed to begin my teaching duties at once, and, as you know, the length of time one has been in a career counts for a great deal. All these reasons seem to me serious, and in themselves sufficient to decide me. But here are others in face of which I could not hesitate. The Bachelor's degree is by no means the simple affair you take it to be, as far, at all events, as concerns obtaining the requisite certificates. I was misinformed as to those preparatory establishments I mentioned to you. They do indeed undertake to give you within a period of five or six months the necessary scientific knowledge to *enable* you to pass the examinations, *provided you have got your certificates elsewhere.* But they do not give certificates on their own account. This has been thoroughly explained to me by Messrs. Galleron and Crouzet, to whom I have spoken on the subject, and who must be better informed thereon than any one else. The only possible means they see would be a certificate of *home* study, whereby my brother would attest my having gone through two distinct twelve months' courses of rhetoric and philosophy *under his eyes*, and which document he would have legalised by the Mayor. But as a matter of fact, I shall never have recourse to this plan. As Mdlle. Ulliac was saying to me yesterday, "Should I, who have sacrificed so much for the sake of uprightness in great matters, do any less for it in small ones?"

Here, then, arises a very great difficulty. Well, dearest Henriette, it all fades away on my entrance here. The Principal has promised that if I enter his service he will get me a special exemption from the Royal Council of Public Instruction, by virtue of which I shall be able to take my Bachelor's degree whenever I choose. And for the higher degrees, the only document I have to be prepared with is my Bachelor's diploma; so once that is obtained I shall be free, and able to take my own time. Lastly, dear Henriette, there is one final reason which appears to me almost in the light of a duty. It is that the arrangement will be eminently pleasing to our mother. We talked of the plan, and she seemed delighted with it. I do not doubt it's still giving her great pleasure. Does it not seem a sort of transition expressly arranged so that nobody's feelings shall be hurt? Nobody can think my removal from St. Sulpice to Stanislas a strange thing. On the contrary, all those I have been formerly associated with have advised it. Nor can any one think it odd that I should move on from Stanislas to some other teaching centre. So everything will pass off quietly. But I am especially delighted on account of my poor dear mother. It is an immense weight off my mind to feel the shock is delayed, and by that means greatly softened. And then she will feel it less when she sees a worldly career opening up before me. What terrified her was the idea of my being "stranded," as she called it, and unable to get any situation; and she used to quote analogous cases to mine which really did make me shiver. This is the origin of my whole line of conduct as regards her, my dear sister. She must have no more idea of anything unusual in my condition than she had before. I am in a state of hesitation; I have made a pause, and I have found a post which permits me to do so with ease and safety, because, in any case, I see an opening before me. This, as it appears to me, is the position we ought to take up before her. And I repeat my conviction that by so doing everything can be arranged without too much suffering for her. I do not know, dear Henriette, if I have succeeded in proving my case for entering the Collège Stanislas to you; for I must confess I have learnt with great pain from Mdlle. Ulliac that it might displease you. Indeed, my dear, I assure you most truthfully, I never would have agreed to do it had I thought this. But, obliged as I was to interpret your supposed wishes, I was convinced the motives I have summed up were more than sufficient to outweigh a trifling dislike, instinctive rather than seriously reasoned. This, too, was Mdlle. Ulliac's decided opinion. She said, "Agree, but make no permanent engagement, and write to Henriette on the subject." This I have done most scrupulously. The great objection is that the college belongs to the Jes——. Oh, dearest sister, it cannot really be possible in this nineteenth century that a clever woman like you should trouble her head about such childishness. As a matter of fact, I have less liking than any one in the world for the Jesuits; indeed, I downright dislike them. But I cannot help laughing heartily at the wild fancy that turns them into a sort of bogey to frighten children with. That, in my eyes, is a very curious psychological fact, which I class with the faculty that invented Bluebeard and a host of other wonderful tales — love of mystery, and an urgent inclination to see it in everything. Some people, I believe, take Eugène Sue's novels for true stories. Oh, my dear, do not let us imitate that folly! The Collège Stanislas is just like any other college. If you read the French newspapers, you must have seen how successful it was in the last great competition. It contains a certain number of priests, especially among the managing staff, but all the masters are ordinary laymen. Enough, dear sister, on this head — though I must say one word more about my relations with the Principal of the college (the Abbé Gratry).

They have been very peculiar, and I am astonished at them my own self. During my first interview I dropped a few words which struck him. Some hours afterwards he sent for me, and a long conversation ensued, during which we came to a perfect understanding. He is a very learned and very remarkable man. He has taken a strong liking to me, and treats me in a way that quite surprises me — all the more because I never really knew any complete confidence arise between myself and another person except after a long period of intercourse during which we were mentally taking stock of each other. I have been perfectly frank and plain-spoken; and note, for it is of capital importance, that it is not as an ecclesiastic that I enter the establishment — no special favour is shown me as such. I should have fought shy of again accepting any on that score. I shall wear ordinary lay dress, and only those I choose to inform on the subject will know what I have been. And now let me say a word of the delightful visit I paid last evening to Mdlle. Ulliac. Oh, my dear sister, how she did delight me! The life that noble-natured woman leads with her mother, modest as it is in all external matters, is exquisitely and ideally beautiful and pure to me. It made me think of my own mother till I could have wept. Yes! that visit marks an epoch in my life! It revealed a whole new sphere of morality and virtue to me. It taught me there is something about womanly virtue which does not exist in man's — something sweet and pure above all other things. She was exceedingly kind to me, and so was her aged mother, who seemed never to tire of talking about you. They have begged me to visit them frequently, and to look on their house as a kind of home. How I thank you, dear sister, for having introduced me to such unpretentious, pure-minded people. It has done me good already. I was so weary of my late insipid intercourse with men whose real character is commonplace in the extreme, in spite of their external appearance of distinction. Here I find every quality at once. I shall call again to-day or to-morrow to take my letter.

To Mdlle. Ulliac, too, I owe a visit I have had to-day from M. Stanislas Julien. He is an excellent fellow, with a very attractive ease and briskness of manner. Unluckily, the presence of a third person inconvenienced us very much. We had to keep to generalities, to promises of special privileges at the Royal Library and that belonging to the institute. But we could not approach the delicate question as to how a young man who *must live by his brains* should set about entering on the career of a teacher of Oriental languages. M. Julien, it seems, can speak with authority on the subject, for he is said to have been in that very position himself. I am to go and see him shortly, to fetch the letters which will secure me the promised library privileges, and then I will touch on the delicate subject. I suffer less now, in my own mind, than I did. The thought of my mother is sad to me, and tender, but it does not agonise me now. The kindness so many people have shown me cheers and supports me. I need to be spoken to gently and sensibly. It is the people without any higher aims who drive me wild. Oh! happy is the man who can think in peace, without worrying himself about his daily bread. Every philosopher ought to come into the world with three thousand francs a year of his own if he lives in Paris, and two thousand in the provinces — not a sou more or less. . . .

Farewell, my dear, kind sister. Write to me very soon, if you have not done it already. Tell me your frank opinion of my new post, and I will follow your advice. Yes, indeed, my sister, on that I am resolved! You know the strength and purity of my love for you! — Your brother and your friend,

E. R.

The fifteen hundred francs will lie untouched. The money our brother has given me is more than enough to defray my preliminary expenses, and I shall have my own quarterly payments. I shall ask your help later on, dear sister; for you will understand the plan of private study is only deferred, and I shall have to come back to it some day if I want to do anything remarkable. But it will be better later.

XXVII

COLLÈGE STANISLAS, *October* 31, 1845.

MY DEAREST HENRIETTE, — Your letter of 11th October reached me only a few hours ago. The idea it gives me, that you may yet be long deprived of news of me, and at a moment of such critical importance to us both, has deeply pained me. I shudder at the thought that you are still under the shadow of the letter I wrote you while I was with our mother, which drew a picture of my then condition as sad as it was faithful. Who can tell whether these lines may not reach your hands before the few I sent immediately on my arrival here, which may indeed have somewhat reassured you. At all events, dear sister, they will have told you how, by the strangest coincidence of circumstances, all my bonds fell from me with a swiftness that fairly astounded me; how I was able at once to take the necessary measures for finding some position suited to our changed plans; and how by the help of kindly disposed persons, and especially through Mdlle. Ulliac, several feasible courses were simultaneously offered me. And my second letter, dearest sister, will have explained that, amongst all these various schemes, the one of settling at the Collège Stanislas was that I most inclined to. I here take up the story of subsequent events, which have reopened a question I had thought completely closed.

This, to begin with, is the exact view I took of my position at the Collège Stanislas. It was, I held, that of a *layman*, yet one which might take on an ecclesiastical shade at will, and I flattered myself I had thus discovered the long-sought solution of my weary problem, viz., to reconcile the imperious rulings of my conscience with the considerations raised by my tenderest affections. Alas! my sister, I was quite mistaken, and I see now I have been trying all along to discover an impossibility. I have only barely escaped finding myself as heavily fettered as before. But have no fear; my story will show you that if you have had reason, up till now, to accuse me of some weakness, I have been firm and resolute this time, even beyond the strictest demands of duty. I was much surprised on reaching the college, to learn from the Superior that I was expected to wear my ecclesiastical habit while performing my duties within its walls. I had no reason to suspect any regulation of the kind, and indeed I had certain precedents before me which warranted my not having any anxiety on the subject. I made a great fight against this extraordinary order; I recalled the frank and straightforward explanation of my sentiments I had given when we were discussing our preliminary arrangements; I instanced certain names even. The answer was couched in such a form as to leave no possibility of immediate answer to a person in my subordinate position. What was I to do? To break matters off then and there, or to enter the college provisionally, and thus to a certain extent to save appearances. I took the latter course. Was I right or wrong? It would puzzle me to answer, even now. But if I did do wrong, it was by stupidity rather than from want of moral sense. For I was firmly resolved to beat a retreat in a very few days if I could not get satisfaction concerning what I felt to be so difficult a matter, and even if I did make a blunder, it will not have done much harm.

A very few days' experience, in fact, convinced me no middle course existed for me between leaving the college and keeping up every appearance of being an ecclesiastic, whence I concluded, clearly and inexorably, that I must not stay on. A day or two later I told the Principal so flatly, and thereupon ensued the strangest intercourse between us two, which gave me the opportunity of making a variety of important psychological observations. I feel my reasoning will have no effect on him, for he is persuaded, and he protests to me that a few months of intellectual communion with him will change my views completely. And knowing the real state of my mind, I cannot press those same reasons of mine too closely on him. So we are both of us very singularly placed. It is as hopeless for us to understand each other as if we were speaking two different languages. Yet he is a very distinguished man: he has his degree of "Docteur-ès-lettres"; he has passed through the École Polytechnique, &c. He strongly urged me to give the matter a practical trial by remaining on temporarily, say, for a few months. But I have barely promised him a few days even. Anyhow, whether I stay on here or not, he has undertaken the necessary steps preliminary to my getting my Bachelor's degree, and he has done me a real service by introducing me to M. Lenormant and M. Ozanam. I shall go up to be examined for my Bachelor's degree by this latter gentleman within *a very few days*.

Really, my dear Henriette, I pause and wonder, when I cast my mind back over the whole of this strange episode! The queerest adventures in the world always come my way, just as if I was born to be worried. But I can assure you the reason I have given is the only one that forces me to leave the college. I am perfectly comfortable here otherwise, and I give up a great deal in thus relinquishing what suits me so perfectly under present circumstances and plunging once more into all the difficulties that tried me so much before, and a successful conclusion to which had appeared so very doubtful. But duty is duty, and I must not shrink from a small sacrifice after having cheerfully made so great a one. Of course I have had to recommence the efforts I had just ceased making to find something in Paris which may enable us to carry out our present programme. I cannot tell you anything definite on that point as yet. But I do not feel the least anxious, because I have the choice of two equally advantageous posts, which cannot both fall through.

The first of these would be under M. Crouzet, Rue des Deux Églises, whom I have already mentioned to you, and with whom I have reopened the negotiations which were broken off when I entered the Collège Stanislas. He now makes me a different offer, and a preferable one, to my mind, though it is less advantageous, financially speaking. He would receive me as an absolutely independent student, stipulating that I should devote an hour and a half every evening to the very small number of students of rhetoric and high mathematics he has in his school, in consideration of which assistance he would only charge me thirty francs a month for my board, and he would even give me a certain amount of private mathematical teaching, which would further equalise the matter. You see I should hold no office in the school; I should be a pupil, and as such no school duties, not even those expected of the teaching staff—such as keeping order, sleeping in the dormitories, &c.—can be required of me. I shall be as free as if I was in furnished lodgings, able to attend any lectures I choose, &c.; only I shall have to give up an hour and a half every day to the school students.

The work I should do with them would be far from being absolutely useless to myself, and even if there was no pecuniary advantage to be gained, I think I should like it for the sake of the service it might be to me, scientifically speaking. A life of thought and deep study, if it is to be really enjoyable and profitable, must have intervals given to some intellectual occupation not too fatiguing nor troublesome in itself. I do not much care about the man himself, that is true enough; but after all, I shall not have much to do with him, so what does it matter? And it strikes me that he is prepared to treat me more as schoolmasters treat their boarders than as they are apt to treat their staff. You know which way the balance turns! I believe he thinks he will gain some pecuniary advantage. All the better for him, and for me too!

The second opening, which would hardly fail me, even if the first were to come to nothing, is a similar arrangement with M. and Mde. Pataud, to whom Mdlle. Ulliac has kindly introduced me. There I should have to give up four hours a day, and even six hours, twice in the week, and I should have the supervision (not a very heavy matter it may be) of ten youths, all of them studying rhetoric or philosophy. As to pecuniary arrangements, I should simply have my board and lodging free. But if you will consider the difference as to hours, and the nature of the duties, you will agree, I am sure, that the other post presents the most advantages. At M. Pataud's I should be an official, obliged to sleep in the dormitory, &c., and barely able to say I have a room of my own.

M. and Mde. Pataud do indeed seem very worthy people. They have been most friendly to me ever since they knew I was your brother, and have spoken of you in the highest terms of regard. I am certain I should be very comfortable with them, and so is Mdlle. Ulliac, who in that refined and witty, but simple, way of hers has made the most indescribable remarks to me on the subject. She vows it is absolutely necessary I should have some such good and kind-hearted woman for my friend. The idea makes me laugh, though not in any scorn. I feel my virtue and good behaviour are safest in my mother's company. And then you must remember the day is coming when *your* presence will be essential to my being, both moral and intellectual. No man should live alone—but is a man alone who has a sister? Do you know, my dearest, we shall hardly recognise each other, intellectually, I mean, when we do meet again! It is through our letters we have grown to know each other so well. Keep your eyes wide open, bodily and mentally too; then you shall tell me all you have seen and felt, and I will tell you all my thoughts, and so shall our life be full of quiet interest and delight.

But to come back to the present time. You see things promise fairly well. The advantages of the two posts I have mentioned are so equal that I shall have no regrets whichever fails me. But I confess the first one tempts me most. Perhaps everything may be decided by to-morrow. A very few days may see me settled in my new surroundings. I am beginning to loathe this provisional state of things.

I am very busy preparing to take my Bachelor's degree at once. I am astonished to find the work so easy; I really am ready to pass now. But I have not got my papers yet. I hope not to have to wait for them beyond the middle of November. In my next letter I will explain the plan of study I propose to follow for taking my higher degrees. This time, dear Henriette, I have confined myself to discussing the solution of our first question—"What temporary position should I take up here to ensure the ultimate realisation of our plans?"

Now to what *special* line (the general direction of my career seems pretty clear) should I devote myself? Here is another question, a still more serious one, no answer to which is possible as yet; and indeed it is not absolutely pressing, for I should have to do what

I am doing now under any circumstances. But I already possess some very important data relative to the subject, obtained from Messrs. Stanislas Julien, Quatremère, and several members of the university whom I have consulted. But as I said, I keep all that for my next letter, in which I shall go into the question fully.

And our poor dear mother? Ah, dear sister, there's the rub! And I can see no help for it. It was on her account especially that I had plumed myself on getting into the Collège Stanislas. What will she say when she hears I have left it! But even my short stay here will have softened matters. This is what I propose doing with regard to her. I will not mention the subject at all till I get my Bachelor's degree. Then I will make her understand the knowledge which suffices for that will not make me a Master of Arts, that special study is requisite, and that one is even expected to attend certain lectures at the Sorbonne, &c., that this cannot be conveniently done from this college — all of it true, to a certain extent. I will manage somehow to put the best appearance on the present state of things; but for Heaven's sake leave it to me, and do not venture to say anything beyond what the gradual course I have marked out admits of. I know, dear sister, you may think my conduct, in several particulars, and especially in this one, betrays some weakness. But you will allow if weakness was ever pardonable, it has been so in my case; not that I apologise for it — I love it, and I glory in it. If ever there lived a bold-hearted man, St. Paul was one, and he said, "I glory in my infirmities." Oh yes! there is a certain holy virtuous weakness, without which something would be lacking to the perfect harmony of man's nature. The perfect man must have some momentary flinching. Do we not see it even in Christ Himself? It is only iron bars that never yield!

As for my mental condition, dear Henriette, it is infinitely calmer than I could have hoped, and there has been no internal revolution to correspond with my exterior ones. I have learnt various things, but the general system of my moral and intellectual life has undergone no change. My tent is larger, but my camping ground is still the same. That departure from "orthodoxy," which has had such a decisive influence on my exterior mode of life, has had but little on my inner one. To me it is a mere change of opinion concerning an important historical point, which does not alter the actual basis of my mental existence in the least. I accept and faithfully hold all my former traditions, practical and speculative, only reserving the right of verifying them by the future results of my own study and meditation. But still I trust those same results will not in future have to be announced to the outer world by means of such a painful rupture as that which has been lately forced upon me!

Farewell, my dear, kind sister. Write to me from Vienna, and give me the necessary instructions for directing my letters to you. I have not yet told you how rejoiced I am to think you are really going to Italy after all. May the journey make your exile seem less hard! And what about France, dear sister? Who knows what the future may have in store! We will cling to each other, and hope still, and let the river of life flow on! It will lead us *somewhere!*

You know how tenderly I love you!

E. RENAN.

XXVIII

To MDLLE. RENAN.

PARIS, *November* 5, 1845.

Although it is only a very few days since I last wrote, I feel I must do so again, my dearest sister, to relate the fresh events which have definitely settled my position here, and to confide all the thoughts that crowd upon me to your sympathetic ear. Never did any situation seem to call for more serious consideration!

Well, dear Henriette, I have formally accepted one of the two posts mentioned in my last, and the very one, too, for which I then avowed my preference. Certain modifications in the original arrangements made it appear still more advantageous. So I have entered M. Crouzet's school in the double capacity of private student and assistant master. But at his request, instead of taking the upper classes only, I have undertaken the lower ones, as far as their Greek work is concerned, the undermaster not having had much practice in that branch of study. To this has been added a private mathematical lesson, to one pupil only, three times a week, and in consideration of these extra duties I have my board and lodging free. The whole of the work put together can never absorb more than two and a half to three hours in each day. And indeed no special time is imposed on me. If I can get through my task any quicker, so much the better for me. Well, having taken up my duties yesterday, I have convinced myself they will never involve my spending the maximum length of time, and I am sure an hour and a half will amply suffice for the evening teaching, without reckoning the mathematical lesson, of course.

I have but seven pupils altogether, so I have no

fear, dear sister, that the performance of my functions will unduly rob me of the time so indispensably necessary for my own purposes just at this juncture. Further, I have no duties as to keeping order in the house, nothing to do with anything that goes on in it; and I am glad of this, for I must admit the school is a very indifferent one. The pupils are miserably backward, and the headmaster himself is far from being a first-rate man. But all that matters little; it is no business of mine to supply them with brains. Material life here, almost the only thing I have to consider, as it is my only object in belonging to the establishment, is very comfortable indeed. I must say, when I consider that M. Pataud asked me to give four and sometimes six hours' teaching a day in return for the same advantages, and with that expected me to sleep in a dormitory, and do without a room of my own, I cannot help thinking the situation I have accepted offers far greater advantages — and that is Mdlle. Ulliac's opinion too. But time will decide the question, anyhow.

As soon as matters get a little clearer for us in one direction they seem to grow complicated in another. The question of my Bachelor's degree is now becoming very serious. Before attempting any steps with regard to the Minister, M. Gratry thought it best to mention the subject to M. Rendu, who is a member of the Royal Council, and the special protector of this establishment. M. Rendu has strongly dissuaded him from taking this course. It would be very difficult, in his view, to get any positive exception made, whatever the motives of such a request might be. The authorities are willing enough not to make too many difficulties, but some appearance of legality there must be; otherwise, as he points out, laws would become a dead letter. No such step could be taken, besides, unless we were perfectly certain of its success; for supposing it failed in its object, every other opening would be closed in future. What would the Minister think, for instance, if a certificate of private study was presented by a M. Renan who, only a few weeks before, had asked to be dispensed from giving any certificate whatever, which fact naturally presupposed he had no special study, either private or university, to show. Several alarming examples of this kind have been quoted to me. M. Rendu held that if I neither could nor would obtain a certificate of private study, the shortest thing for me would be to enter myself at some college for *two years*, and to do it as soon as possible, so that this present year might count. How shameful it all is, dear Henriette. How absurd to hold a young man responsible for the place where his fate has set him, without ever considering how much he may have struggled against it. But this is no time for argument, dear sister; we are face to face with facts, and sadly real ones, alas! What is to be done? The idea of a certificate of private study was excessively distasteful to me, in the first instance, especially on account of the difficulty in which it would place Alain. You know, of course, he would have to get it legalised by the Mayor of the district. And then the straightforwardness of the plan itself struck me as doubtful. Certain very strictly upright people have endeavoured to remove these scruples. It is an undoubted fact that the real value of these certificates is very well known, and that the untruth, if such there is, lies in the form only. Nobody is really taken in, and the persons who accept the certificates are perfectly aware that three parts of them are false as far as their form goes. The law has allowed of this loophole to lessen the odium such brutal exclusiveness would bring with it, and so true is this, that the regulations are worded so as evidently to denote the intention of permitting the equivocation whenever reason and good sense demand it. Thus, whenever I mention my scruples, everybody laughs at me. For deceit ceases to be deceit as soon as the formula used is one which, though false in itself, is universally accepted as its real value. Now this "private study" has grown to be synonymous with any study prosecuted elsewhere than at the university, *with the consent of the student's relatives*. What does it matter, after all, whether my father or brother has had me taught philosophy under his own eye by this tutor or that, or sent me to receive instruction in some establishment selected by him? And my case is really so pressing and the injustice of it so crying, that I do not feel justified in denying myself a freedom all other people take, and which really seems tacitly and intentionally granted by the originator of the law. I have therefore written to Alain. But you may imagine, dear sister, how uncomfortable it makes me to ask the poor fellow to do such a thing. I have besought him, if he thinks anything disagreeable is likely to ensue for him, to tell me so frankly, and do nothing more in the matter. There is no doubt that when the authorities are sensible people, they never do make the slightest difficulty. And the Mayor's signature is quite unquestioned. No inquiries are ever made as to the truth of his assertion, especially when the examination takes place in a different academy from that in which the private study is supposed to have taken place. I was afraid, indeed, for some time I might have to apply at Rennes, in virtue of my having studied at St. Malo. But careful inquiries from the Secretary to the Faculty of Letters have shown this to be unnecessary, and that the whole thing can be settled between the Sorbonne and the Minister on the presentation of a petition to this last by the Dean of the Faculty. This is a mere formality, in the way of which no difficulty ever crops up. But unfortunately it always takes a long time. I shall think myself most fortunate if I contrive to pass my examination within a month. This tries my patience terribly. All these tiresome preliminaries will have cost me ten times the trouble and anxiety the actual preparation for the examination has given me. If I could only be sure of seeing the reward of my pains! I await our brother's letter with the greatest anxiety.

A fresh anxiety is on me now, dear Henriette, and a far worse one, for it goes straight to my heart instead of to my brain, and you are its object. In her little note, Mdlle. Ulliac spoke of your health as being *very much shaken*. I hurried off at once to ask for an explanation of this terrible reticence on her part, and the most dreadful secrets were confided to me. What, Henriette, my dearest, you have been in suffering, and we knew nothing of it! Ought you to have hidden it from me, at all events? I can understand your concealing it from our mother—but *me !* Listen, dearest sister; I am going to tell you something serious, my firm resolve, the outcome of my long talk with Mdlle. Ulliac, of the *league*, as she calls it, we have entered into, she and I. You are to choose between two things. Either your travels in Italy will lead you back to France, and thus be part of your return journey — for you shall never leave us again, be sure of that — or else you will go no further; you will leave the Zamoyskys in that lovely country, and come home to us in the spring. Do you hear, my dear one? This is a settled matter, immutable, irrevocable. So bid an eternal farewell to the scenes you are passing through, and yield yourself up to the exquisite joy the certainty your exile is nearly over must inspire.

I can fancy all the objections your unselfish devotion will raise against our fiat. Oh! why cannot I convince you, as I am convinced myself, that it is the very depth of your devotion which should drive you back and keep you with us. Your health cannot stand the strain, that much is clear; and without you, my poor dear sister, what would become of me? My God, I shudder at the thought! It took hold of me the moment I read that fatal note from Mdlle. Ulliac, and never shall I forget the fearful nightmare it has been to me. Henriette, what would my present — above all, what would my future — be without you? I hereby assure you that the instant I lose you I bid farewell to every interest in my life, which will thenceforth be colourless, strengthless, springless utterly. In a word, I shall be driven to moral suicide. How often, great Heaven, have I been tempted to it already, and the thought of you has saved me, and made me feel life was good, and bade me cling to it! I should grow selfish, oh my sister, with the most horrible kind of selfishness! Ah, save me from that miserable fate! Think of it, dearest Henriette. Remember my life is bound up with yours, and then you must surely realise the tenderest mark of affection you can give me is to live on for my sake!

You will say there are pecuniary difficulties to be feared. Dear one, let me reason with you on that point too. To begin with, I cannot think such great people would let you depart empty-handed and without any provision for your future; that would be unheard of. And further, seeing I earn my board and lodging now, I am not likely to lose ground next year, especially as I shall have taken my degrees by then. A man with a Master's degree cannot fail to find a good post, or, at all events, what will lead to one. I have many acquaintances in the professorial circle who will be very useful to me. Messrs. Julien, Quatremère, Galleron, and Guihal all take the greatest interest in me. I owe my present situation to M. Galleron. M. Guihal has promised to provide for me when once I have taken my degrees; and besides, dear sister, I have plans of my own, which I will enter into later on. At all events, I have confident hope of being able to support myself in future, and of being in a position to add my quota to our common fund before two years are out, and that without prejudicing my future or deadening my best intellectual powers in any way.

And again, my dearest Henriette, I am sure you have no idea of living in utter idleness when you return, nor would your personal tastes permit it. Mdlle. Ulliac has mentioned several schemes, one more excellent than the other. There was only one I did not greatly care about, that of teaching in a school, and I must admit she told me it appeared highly improbable to her. Let us keep clear of all that sort of thing, in Heaven's name! but she spoke of your giving public lectures for young girls. A splendid notion that; and of a newspaper for young people, too — that would be better still. Mdlle. Ulliac has reputation, friends, every qualification, I may say, that such an undertaking would demand. She talks of it all with the most eager and infectious enthusiasm, but she wants you, Henriette; she can do nothing, she declares, without your help. Come back to us, then, my dearest. I will supply you with any amount of material — Greek, Latin, Hebrew, philosophical, philological, theological even, if you so desire.

U

I make over all my work to you in fee simple. Only come back to us; that is my *delenda Carthago*. It shall be the burden of every letter of mine until I have convinced you utterly.

Ah! never shall I forget that evening on the 2nd of November, when Mdlle. Ulliac opened my eyes. Alas! my Henriette, how you have suffered. And she sat and told me all about it here in Paris, and I — I stood staring with surprise. Nothing but our tender care can ever make amends for all you have endured for us, dear love. We will "nurse you up," as our good friend puts it. Yes, yes, indeed, dear Henriette, it is high time your loving heart should be surrounded by hearts which throb responsive to it. It is high time, indeed, your wearied, worn-out frame should rest awhile amidst the beings for whose sake you have undergone so much; and yet another reason which has long pressed upon my mind, and which Mdlle. Ulliac also insists on greatly — the politico-religious condition of Poland. I could not speak of it while you were there, but often, when I read the papers, I shivered at the thought that my Henriette lived in such surroundings. You will apprehend my meaning without another word from me. Whoever else goes there, no French-woman ever can return.

I come back to the financial side of the question,

for there, I fear, you will make the hardest fight; but even supposing we had to begin by struggling hard for our living, the future would make up for that. Mdlle. Ulliac seems to command everything except funds. Well, what is there to prevent our selling our little patrimonial inheritance should that prove necessary? Our two shares put together would bring in a certain amount, and our mother would be quite content if she saw it would lead to your settling down amongst us. That thought always overrules every other in her mind, and my next letter shall tell you of all the plans she has woven to bring it to pass. And then, dear Henriette, Alain really loves us; he would help us now and then, at all events. Come then, my dearest, try and take a brighter view of things. Should we not put some faith, too, in the Ruler of the Universe, He whom we have been taught to call our Father. "Behold the fowls of the air: they sow not, neither do they reap; yet your heavenly Father feedeth them. Are ye not much better than they? Consider the lilies of the field: they toil not, neither do they spin: and yet I say unto you, that even Solomon in all his glory was not arrayed like one of these. If God so clothe the grass of the field, which to-day is, and to-morrow is cast into the oven, shall He not much more clothe you, oh ye of little faith?"

And I say it again, my sister; here is the most solid and truthful of all my reasons — remember this is a question of life and death to you, and so to me.

I will not speak just yet, dear sister, either of my schemes for the less immediate future, or of the plan of study I have laid out. I must have more information before either can be absolutely decided upon. I am regularly attending the examinations now going on at the Sorbonne for Bachelor's degrees, both in arts and science (merely as a spectator, of course), so as to calculate my own chances of success. Yesterday I took possession of my little room. It is a very pleasant one. It gets all the fresh air from the Luxembourg quarter of the town. There is a delightful view over the Luxembourg itself, the observatory, parks, gardens, and Mdlle. Ulliac's little square house away in one corner. The grounds of the Deaf and Dumb Institute are under my windows. My chief recreation is to watch the poor little inmates at their play.

So at last, dear Henriette, I am placed just as you would have me. You know how perfectly my own tastes are suited here. My loneliness is my only trial. But then I shall soon have you back. A few months will fly by very swiftly — that is all I reckon for, dear sister! Sometimes, in the evening especially, I have moments of unutterable sadness, when I think of my mother — of you, my Henriette — of my simple, happy past — and when I look out on the cold world around me, so indifferent to divine truth, and so incapable of understanding it. And then it is so dreary to feel one is only perched upon a bough, and soon to take flight again. How well I now understand the truth of what you once said to me about a roving life. Man's instinct is to settle down, to take root wherever he may go, and when the rapidity of travelling forbids his doing so, he suffers in the end. Habit is such a pleasant thing, and habit can only be formed where one has time to settle and pitch one's tent. Now I really begin to realise how trying your life must have been these past ten years. And how different it is from mine! My situation is exceedingly easy and pleasant in itself, while yours ... Heavens! when I think of it! How joyful that day will be which brings you back to home and all its sweetness! We shall be so happy together, my dear! I really am naturally very gentle and good-tempered. You will let me lead my own simple, thoughtful life, and I will pour out all my ideas and feelings to you. And we will have friends too, noble in mind and pure in life, to brighten ours. You see, dear sister, I paint my dream of happiness in the fairest colours. Remember if you fail me, it must crumble into dust!

Farewell, my dear, good sister. The fruition of the hopes I live on lies in the hollow of your hand. You know what it all hangs on! I like to think of your Italian journey — it should be both pleasant and profitable for your health, it seems to me. But as you may fancy, its chief beauty in my eyes lies in the part that brings you nearer home. Pray write me often from your various stopping places. The distance between us seems nothing to me now. At all events our letters will not be months in transit, let us hope. Lean on my love just as I do on yours. — Your brother, your friend,

E. RENAN.

Our poor mother took the news of my having entered the Collège Stanislas very well, and what makes it more remarkable, she believed I was entered as a layman. We are really getting on, but we must be exceedingly careful. Do not let her know I have left the college. Your journey in Italy, and above all, your return to France, will put other things out of her head. And then I paint the future gaily to her. Would that I could ensure her happiness! Imagine my anguish when I thought I should have to make her wretched for ever! Happily, things have grown clearer, and I hope future joy will atone for passing pain. By a sudden turn of the wheel,

M. Dupanloup and all his close adherents have left the little seminary. He has doubtless undergone what every superior-minded man belonging to that body is certain to endure.

XXIX

To Mdlle. Renan.

Paris, *December* 15, 1845.

I write these lines, dear sister, in a state of extreme anxiety. I cannot understand your long silence, and I wear myself out in trying to guess at some explanation which may somewhat lessen my alarm. We ought to have had a letter from Vienna more than a month ago. Have you left that town? Is your letter lost in that weary post? Did some unexpected event retard your journey, or stop it altogether? These are the hypotheses on which I prefer to dwell. But when I think of your already failing health, of the sufferings you concealed from me for so long, then, oh my dearest sister, I get into a perfect agony of fear. My imagination conjures up every sort of terror. I fancy you, my sister, my best and dearest friend, suffering, worn out with pain, far from your own country and from those who love you best.

If this should be the case, I do beseech you, dearest Henriette, in the name of our common affection, to let me know without delay, and I will fly to you at once. No sacrifice is worth thinking about under such circumstances. Let me know everything, my dear sister, without restriction or reserve. The day when you might have feared the knowledge of your suffering would have a baneful influence on me, by driving me yet further on the path I then was following, is gone by for ever. Its only present effect will be to spur me onwards, and urge me to fresh exertions to put an end to your discomforts.

Mdlle. Ulliac is the only person to whom I can confide my anxiety, and her fears double mine, for she is better informed than I about the sad subject of your physical suffering. Oh! what a weight it would be off my mind to learn my Henriette is still spared to us, and travelling joyously and happily back to France. Yes! back to France, my dearest, never to leave it! Of course the thought of your seeing Italy delights me; but the great charm of the journey, in my eyes, is that I look on it as a pleasant roundabout way of returning to your own country. I have said it once, and I still maintain it, you *cannot* go back to Poland. But then, kind Heaven, how can I tell you are not in Poland still? Positively, I do not know exactly what corner of Europe holds the being towards whom my thoughts so fondly turn. I am absolutely at sea as to where this letter will find you, and I have only put off sending it till now, because I thought it would not catch you at Vienna. Oh if I only get that thrice blessed letter to-morrow, or the day after! But I have delayed writing for so many days in the hope of hearing from you, that I fear if I put off sending this any longer I shall cause you the same anxiety as that which now devours me.

I have not the courage, in my present painful state of tension, to enter into a calm discussion of the important schemes which fill my thoughts whenever they are not claimed by a much tenderer interest. But I must give you a slight sketch of the chief events that have taken place since our last communications, and tell you the effect they have had upon my mind. From this out — moving about as you will constantly be — we may not be able to keep up any regular correspondence for some considerable time. First let me tell you, once for all, dear sister, that I am very comfortable here, and that, for a temporary arrangement, I really could not have hoped for anything better. Experience confirms every one of my original opinions. The head of the school is a very worthy man, not distinguished either in intellect or sentiments. In that he resembles the large majority of his kind. I confess my first experience of actual intercourse with men has brought me much disappointment. Hitherto I have judged them conjecturally, supposing them to possess certain qualities. Facts have convinced me I had taken them to be more acute and intellectual than they really are. At first I fancied they were all phœnixes, and I measured every step I made and every word I spoke with all the caution of a novice. Now I have gauged the people round me, I am beginning to feel more firm upon my feet. I know my manner is not like other people's. But I will not try to alter it; it is natural to me, and it answers very well.

The consideration shown me here is really surprising, all the more as the gentleman at the head of affairs is not considerate to people in general. But as you know, everything depends on the attitude one takes up at first, and every one can, more or less, dictate the tone to be taken with himself. When I was negotiating with the proprietor here, I suggested his making inquiries about me from my old masters at St. Nicolas. He went there, and they told him every kind of marvel about me. All this has done me wonderful service. I get on just as well with the pupils, and do not foresee having any difficulty with them. I already have private teaching, three times a week only, which brings me in five-and-twenty francs a month, and I hope to get some more. But all this is mere sport, my dearest. I cannot take any of these trifles seriously. Let us talk — ah! let us talk about our future!

The particular direction my career should ultimately take has never been a doubtful point with you, dear sister. From the very instant when we first began to turn over all these serious matters together, I told you clearly it must be one of those I should describe as intellectual. But as you will feel, this word implies a considerable latitude of choice, and a wide field for my indecision consequently offered. Circumstances have narrowed that, and, as we have often agreed, it has reduced itself to two alternatives, the study of Oriental languages, or entrance at the university. I have, therefore, had to consider what advantages and chances of subsequent success each of these two courses presented to me. I began by making inquiries about Oriental languages, towards which you seemed to me to have a certain leaning, and I had the great good-fortune of being able to collect the necessary evidence from the lips of the very men most capable of giving pertinent judgment on the subject. As I had an introduction from the Hebrew professor at the seminary, and was a former pupil of his own as well, I was able to confer with M. Quatremère, and by good Mdlle. Ulliac's friendly offices, aided by you, my sister, the good genius who guides me everywhere I go, I gained access to M. Stanislas Julien. I was much struck by the perfect harmony between the opinions of these two gentlemen, and the absolute similarity of their conclusions. It was almost as if they had agreed beforehand, and this singular coincidence, added to the consummate wisdom of their remarks, gave them unquestioned authority in my eyes.

Each of them, while pressing me, with all the zeal of a savant for his own special department of science, to continue that particular line of study, told me frankly I should be very foolish to build any hopes for the near future on my efforts. These studies are so out of the common order, in fact, that they only pave the way to a very small number of openings. Will you believe that when I looked into the matter I found there is only *one* professorial chair in the whole of France, that actually held by M. Quatremère, in which the languages I have studied, and which I still desire to study, viz., the ancient languages of the East, might eventually place me. Now M. Quatremère *has already adopted* his future successor in the person of M. Emmanuel Latouche, nephew of the Abbé Latouche, whose acquaintance I made at M. Quatremère's lectures; and if there were any possibility of competing with him, even in spite of the fact of his having been chosen by his predecessor, I should not like to look as if I were supplanting any one.

The modern Oriental languages do indeed offer more choice as to ultimate employment. There are professorships at the Collège de France and at the School for Oriental Languages attached to the Bibliothèque Royale, and then there are consulships, interpreterships, and so forth. As to the professorial chairs, they are occupied, and seem likely to be so, as M. Julien naïvely remarks, for a long while yet. The other posts mentioned have no scientific character, and are evidently not the kind of thing we want. And besides, the modern Oriental tongues do not bring nearly so rich results to the student as the ancient ones; and I really could not make up my mind to devote my life to studies which would have no higher aim than the facilitation of commercial relations in some shape or other.

The practical advice both these gentlemen gave me was to continue my Oriental studies quietly, but to take up some other ostensible career to supply temporary needs, thus leaving myself free to embrace any opportunity which may arise. They went over all the most famous Oriental scholars of the day, and pointed out to me that all of them, except those whose private means permitted them to study as amateurs, had followed this course. It shall be mine too, my dearest, as to the two first points at all events; for as to the last, I shall very likely never make any effort to create a position based on that particular portion of my general knowledge.

But learning of every kind has its value, and these languages will have all the more in my case, because I shall be almost the only member of the university who knows much about them. Now there is a huge vein of information as to the affinity of these Eastern tongues with the classics which has been left utterly unworked, thanks to the profound ignorance of our most eminent Greco-Latinists. There are several gaps, too, in the teaching at the Collège de France which will necessitate the founding of new professorships, the holders of which must be intimately acquainted with the languages in question, so as to be able to lecture on Comparative Philology, Biblical Exegesis, Hebrew Literature, and Poetry, none of them included in the ordinary Hebrew course, which is purely grammatical in its nature. I have work ready on these subjects which I believe to be new, and which is susceptible of further and interesting development. The Collège de France is so constituted that professorships are not difficult to create for persons who bring forward new and advanced ideas, provided these are not supposed to pertain to the domain of any existing chair. These are only dreams, dear sister, but I want to show you the study in question may be of great ultimate service to me, even in external matters, and that there is no reason I should regret the time I have devoted to it.

The Oriental languages being thus eliminated from my programme, no choice remained to me. I was bound to turn every thought and every effort towards the university. I will not here enumerate the various difficulties and aversions which might have made me shrink, since necessity drives me to overlook them all. I may even say frankly that the university does not greatly tempt me, that the instruction given there is not as purely scientific as I could wish, that I only endure the classical work because it is my sole means of securing the right of independent study, that classical subjects, as a rule, are not to my taste, &c., &c. But all the same, I have absolutely resolved to take up this line, especially as none of the drawbacks I have mentioned are insuperable. But to which side of university teaching shall I apply myself? Here is a far more difficult and debatable problem! The system of instruction is divided up into four principal branches or examination classes: 1st, Classical Literature; 2nd, History; 3rd, Philosophy! 4th, Mathematics and Physical Science. The first three constitute the Faculty of Arts; the last, subdivided for examination purposes into Mathematical, Physical, and Natural Science, the Faculty of Science. The examinations are so arranged that no man can pass in one section of a Faculty unless he is very strong in the two others. Thus, for example, the tests for a Philosophy Fellowship are exactly the same, except in the case of the last one, as those for a History Fellowship. As a result of this arrangement the only choice is the one between the two Faculties, and that indeed has been the subject of a mighty controversy within me.

Science has such a charm for me; I rank it so much higher than literature, *quâ* literature, that I doubted long as to whether I would not give myself up to it entirely. And I may add, without presumption, I was morally certain in that case of rising very high in time, that branch of study being less crowded, and free from certain peculiarities which at times render the other almost antipathetic to me. But the one thing, alas! to which it could not possibly lead me is philosophy. And philosophy it is that has made me elect for literature, and overridden the otherwise powerful considerations that had given me pause. I could never be satisfied, intellectually speaking, with a chair of physical science, however brilliant its surroundings. Physical science is not everything in life, and what is the use of learning unless a man learns to know his own nature and his God — without philosophy, in short!

No study which excludes all others has any fascination for me. There is only one, the queen of all the rest, which sums them up and crowns them, which treats alike of God and of man's soul, and of his reason, to which I can devote myself completely. I am far from thinking philosophy as it is publicly taught, as it must indeed be taught, answers to the description I have just given; but it is the branch of university teaching which approaches my ideal most closely, so I was bound to take it up. Often have I cursed the system under which my beloved study is overshadowed by and connected with others which are not even closely related to it! To my mind (which is much more inclined to science than to literature) philosophy should either have a separate Faculty of its own, or be incorporated in the Faculty of Science. But while feeling I must make a virtue of necessity, I am inclined to think a great many of the subjects which are here combined with philosophy not at all unsuited to my particular intelligence, nor unlikely to be of service to me. History and advanced literary criticism, as I find them in the works of Kant, Schlegel, &c., are quite as dear to me as downright philosophy, of which they really are a certain form.

x

The one thing I find it hard to swallow is that pedantic rhetoric for which our university men entertain a respect, to my thinking, almost laughable. To many of them, I really do believe, the maker of the most highly polished of those dull harangues on which students of rhetoric are always sharpening their schoolboy wit is the greatest man upon this earth! I nearly fainted when I had to drag all those old classical rags out of their dusty seclusion. How cold and empty it all is when once one has sipped the wondrous nectar of the only living science!

Let me get back to hard facts, dear sister. The means of getting a fellowship have occupied my mind as much as the question of which Faculty I was to study for. There can be no doubt the surest and most brilliant plan is to enter the École Normale; so as soon as I was free to do it, I set about collecting all the information I could get, and to make assurance doubly sure I made it my business to see the Principal himself. He received me very well, and the simplicity with which I told him my story seemed to please him. That you must know, dear Henriette, is the inevitable preamble, for the first question every one asks me is, "Where I have been educated." It has struck me wherever I go that the word St. Nicolas, *coupled with the name of Dupanloup*, produces an excellent effect. The Principal (M. Vacherot), with an obliging kindness which delighted me, gave me the fullest information and all the necessary lists, &c., and added a few significant words about the extreme liberal-mindedness of the university authorities, who, so he averred, would jump at the opportunity of proving the university does not repudiate persons whose education has not been altogether moulded on academic lines.

. . . .

There are many pros and cons about this matter of entering the École Normale. It terrifies me to think a period of three years, added to a year of preparation, must elapse before I can cease being a burden on those I love, and to whose support I am so anxious to contribute as soon as may be. Think, dearest sister, must I wait four more years, till I am seven-and-twenty, before I can even begin to repay all you have done for me? On the other hand, supposing I took my degrees without entering the École Normale, even granting (which I think unlikely) I had to wait so long, I might hope to ease the pecuniary burden of the delay by various temporary expedients.

And then, my dearest, does not the idea of being tied for ten years frighten you, as it does me? Supposing the wind blew from some unexpected quarter, supposing some lucky opportunity came my way, and I was bound hand and foot inexorably? not to mention, what you will doubtless feel, that a certain passive obedience would be expected of me, which involves a certain risk of constraint, both as to individual taste and intellectual development. Several instances of this have been quoted to me. And again, though the outcome of my solitary studies may have a strongly individual stamp, and so be less suited to the views of those who will have to judge it, there will be all the more independence and originality about it, and at all events, it will not be cast in the common mould, a thing I dread more than anything on earth.

In a word, dear sister, if I keep my personal independence, I shall have a far wider field of intellectual action. For instance, I already have the outlines, or, at all events, the germs, of various works, quite original as to their point of view, which I should like to carry through, and which if they were ultimately submitted to competent authorities might lead to something more. Nothing would be easier than this, once I have obtained my Master's degree, at any rate, supposing I carry on my studies by myself. But if I enter the École Normale, any idea of that kind must be indefinitely deferred. The one really considerable advantage I can see about that step is the position it undoubtedly gives you in the eyes of others, and the acquaintances it naturally procures you without any effort or intrigue on your part.

Simple and retiring as I am by nature, it is a great trial to me to have to endeavour to put myself forward. In an isolated position, with all its drawbacks, with no central body to assist me, I should have to try and make myself known, to attract attention, in fact, in quarters whence I may look for ultimate support. A situation which is naturally within the general view, and which by the very fact of one's holding it attracts men's eyes, is surely much to be preferred.

As to the entrance examination and my chances of success in it, here, dear sister, is my plain opinion. Though want of confidence in my own powers is not my usual failing, I confess I cannot look forward to this trial of them without a certain amount of alarm. It is easier than the examination for the Master's degree evidently, for students who have passed it are supposed to give up a year or two afterwards to preparation for that. Now my idea, if I do not get into the École Normale, would be to go up for my degree in a year's time. All the more reason, say you, for my not being afraid of the entrance examination. Not at all, dear sister. The maxim that the greater strength presupposes the lesser has no point in this case, because the tests are different in their nature, especially as regards the written work, which constitutes the really difficult and important portion of them.

The essays for the degree examination are critical and philosophical dissertations quite in accord with my turn of mind. Those required at the entrance examination, on the contrary, are rhetorical compositions, to which I have always felt the greatest repugnance. Besides this, the candidates for admission are most of them young men, fresh from their rhetorical and philosophical lectures, and full of the ardour of youth. I am old already, and I cannot but laugh at their schoolboy fervour. However, everything depends on the nature of the subject given out, and I think it will be one I shall be able to discuss with considerable success by treating it from my own particular point of view. As to my *vivâ voce*, I have no fears. I am more than equal to all that.

In spite of my hesitation between these various reasons, all of which have so much weight, there can be no doubt as to my line of conduct. My preparatory work must, in fact, be much the same, whether I propose to enter the École Normale or go up at once for my degree. My decision would make but little change in my actual practice. So we have plenty of time to make up our minds and prosecute further inquiries. I have just discovered that one of my old classmates is actually at the École Normale. I intend to go and see him within the next few days, and to ask him for information which will doubtless prove interesting. Further, I have lately, through one of my old schoolfellows and best friends at St. Sulpice, and his near relation, made the acquaintance of M. Feugère, Professor of Rhetoric at the Collège Henri IV. (whose pupils here I overlook). There was some idea at first of his giving me instruction in my preparatory work; but he did not care to undertake this regularly and consequently accept remuneration for doing it, which had been the original plan as arranged between my St. Sulpice friend and myself. He has agreed, however, very willingly, to give me all the assistance I need, and has advised my doing any I choose of the papers he sets his pupils, all of which pass through my hands, he undertaking to look them over and correct them. For regular "coaching" he has recommended me to apply to M. Egger, Professor of Greek Literature at the Sorbonne, a celebrated Greek scholar, who has established special lectures for students preparing for entrance or degree examinations, and not belonging to the École Normale.

I forthwith called on M. Egger, to whom M. Feugère had already been good enough to mention me privately. Unluckily his lecture is limited by the authorities to fifteen students, and the number is full. But I am sure of the first vacancy. It will cost us a hundred francs a year, but I really believe the money could not be laid out better. A still more important point is that M. Egger is also lecturer (professor) at the École Normale, and consequently a member of the board of admission.

I run on, dear sister, and yet there are so many more things I might tell you. I forgot to say that everything is settled about the papers for my Bachelor's degree. My brother sent me those I asked him for, and no difficulty was made when they were sent in to the Sorbonne. But the fact of my having studied in the university district of Rennes has necessitated a special permission from the Ministry of Education for me to pass my examination in Paris. Hence arise long formalities, which are tedious, but nothing more. I daily expect to hear I am called up for my examination.

Your good angel, dear sister, has been my guide again in this affair at the Ministry. I happened upon a very excellent worthy man, M. Soulice, who has a most affectionate recollection of you. Mdlle. Ulliac recommended me to him, and he has rendered me some valuable help. Without it I should have been terribly hindered. As it is, the delay at the longest cannot last beyond the first of January. My preparation is quite complete, and has not cost me any very great labour.

My exact address is

8 *Rue des Deux Églises.*

This is what the École Normale supplies. There can be no doubt that any man who distinguishes himself there may go on steadily and peacefully with his work, without what I will call that collar-gall of everyday anxieties from which no philosophy can legitimately free us. It is clear enough that even if I become the most learned savant of the day nobody will seek me out and obtain advancement for me, unless I take care to let others know my powers. Learning is written on no man's brow. It must be constrained to reveal itself, and that revelation is torture unless it is the natural consequence of the student's external position. As to my actual work, dear Henriette, I reserve all details for my next letter; this one has reached a most alarming length already. I am closely attending all the lectures at the Sorbonne and at the Collège de France which are like to assist me in my present undertaking. The Sorbonne courses are more interesting and spirited this year than usual, public attention, which had been temporarily diverted elsewhere, having been recalled to them by the daily press. And then, as an effect of the interruptions at the Collège de France (spontaneous perhaps, though carefully led up to by M. Michelet and M. Quinet), the noisy, stirring popular student element, which attends lectures merely to clap its hands and drum with its feet and shout, has been driven back to the Sorbonne.

The Sorbonne may have gained in numbers, but it has not improved as to orderliness, and its peaceful walls have witnessed scenes unheard of in its annals. I was present myself during M. Lenormant's lectures at the most indescribably disgraceful sights, typical of this nineteenth century of ours. This professor, whom I know to be a man of remarkably liberal views (though I am far from personally adopting all his opinions), was interrupted, all through his lectures, by coarse invectives and frantic noise, nobody quite knew why. It was evidently a plot among the ringleaders to drive him from his professorial chair, and force the authorities to reinstate M. Quinet. They kept shouting for M. Quinet as if he had been there to answer them. If you ever see the French papers, some echo of this students' quarrel will have reached you.

Good God! dear Henriette! I keep drowsing on with this long tale of mine, and now a cruel thought breaks on its quiet peace! It may be, even as I write, that you are lying in suffering and exhaustion! too ill to read these lines perhaps! Compare the dates, dear sister. This is the 16th of December, and in your last, dated 28th October, you seemed to hold out hopes of my hearing very soon again. I wait — ah! in what agonies of impatience do I wait! The daily post-hour is an anxious moment to me. My mother and Alain share my alarm.

Our dear mother is well, and I am glad to notice she has had opportunities of making little trips to Lannion and Guingamp, which have amused her. She still believes me at the Collège Stanislas, and I shall not be able to make any acceptable excuse for having left it until I have taken my Bachelor's degree; so pray be careful, if you mention me, to keep that fact in view. There lies the incurable wound, dear sister, and I cannot think of it without the most poignant anguish. It needs all my strength of will to keep me from dwelling on it. Our brother gives me the kindliest encouragement and support. He has made his own inquiries about the École Normale, and strongly urges my entrance. I have paid him over the 1500 francs from Rothschild, which I have no earthly need of now. He has opened an account for me at Mallet Frères, in case of any sudden need. This seems to me the better plan. *Our* funds are thus in safety, and bearing interest.

Mdlle. Ulliac is quite well. I saw her a few days ago. She awaits a letter from you before writing again. Mde. Ulliac is in a very poor way. They both of them show me the greatest kindness and affection. My weekly dissipation is to go to their mesmeric séances; the chief charm of which, as far as I am concerned, lies, I confess, in the society I meet there. Although I have been the subject of some personal experiments, I am less of a believer than when I first began. If to this exciting recreation you add my Sunday evening visit to the reading-room to look over the week's newspapers, the full tale of my amusements lies before you.

Farewell, you best of friends, on whose faithful heart mine leans so thankfully in its hours of weakness! O Henriette, how I need your presence! I beseech you, for Heaven's sake, take care of your health, and think of me, whose life would be an utter desert if I lost you. Oh! if you knew the castles I build, and could see how you fill them all! Farewell, my dear, farewell!

ERNEST RENAN.

XXXII

PARIS, *December* 25, 1845.

I can bear it no longer, dear Henriette. I am writing to Mde. Catry, beseeching her to tell me the real truth. I must rid myself of this agonising doubt which tortures me as much almost as the most crushing certainty. Henriette, dearest Henriette! what is the matter? You have been delayed on your journey, I tell myself — you have stopped somewhere in Galicia. But surely letters are delivered in every

European country. I go wild with terror when I think that the frightful nightmares my fancy sometimes conjures up may after all be hideous facts! Our mother, too, is terribly anxious. Mdlle. Ulliac knows not what to think. I count the days till I can have Mde. Catry's answer. Good God! suppose I have to wait till then! If I even knew where to find you, where to turn to get direct news of you! but I am utterly in the dark. Who knows whether even Mde. Catry will be able to tell me anything! Oh! if only some good news puts an end to my anxiety, how heartily I will swear that this time shall be the last, and these terrible separations never cause us torture more! France! France! dear sister! That is settled and irrevocable! I should feel I was trifling with the life of my beloved sister if I allowed her to risk it on my account a moment longer. I have a strange and unexpected piece of news to give you. It would be a great delight to me were it not for the miserable anxiety which darkens everything. Oh! how joyfully should I announce it, if only some good report of you would arrive to set my mind at rest. The simple fact is this:—

While I was lecturing on Hebrew at St. Sulpice I drew up for my own guidance a very full set of notes, which form a pretty complete Hebrew grammar, on a plan which is, to my mind, both novel and original—

so at least those who heard my lectures thought it. My former Hebrew master, who is still my very good friend, asked to see these notes, and thought them so good that he has strongly pressed me to publish them. I should not, I confess, have thought of doing so yet, but he answered my objections by such advantageous offers that I was really forced to give in, at all events for the moment. First of all, he undertakes to get *his* publisher (for he writes himself) to accept the work as *his own*, leaving me all the proprietary rights in the book. Further, and this is the chief point, he being in charge of the Hebrew studies in all the seminaries connected with the Society of St. Sulpice, assures me he will have the work adopted as the teaching manual in all those establishments, and there is really no work at present in existence which fully supplies that need. You will understand the vital importance of this last clause. I confess it has dazzled me, and I could not find it in my heart to refuse. And indeed, dear sister, I have so many ideas on the subject which seem to me both novel and correct, I have collected so much material, and my research has resulted in so much interesting matter, that I have no doubt of complete success.

All the students who attended my lectures thought so highly of them, that they took the trouble of copying out these same notes in full, in spite of their being so voluminous. I have enriched my repertory since then with a number of fresh facts. In short, I shall throw my whole soul and strength into the work, and I feel I shall win success. You will readily conceive what an invaluable start in life this would give me. A book is the best kind of introduction to the learned world. Its very composition necessitates consulting a number of wise men, who are never more flattered than by the homage their knowledge thus receives. The dedication, again, may secure one friends and protectors in high places. My idea would be to dedicate my book to M. Quatremère. I have quantities of facts and work on this and kindred subjects for which there is no room in any grammar, large as my conception of that word is; and I have no doubt that once I can put this information into literary form it may find a place in the columns of some one of the scientific publications which treat specially of Asiatic subjects. I do not enumerate all the advantages this would bring, dear sister. You will see them for yourself. I must tell you, by the way, that the work itself is nearly finished; and were it not that I desire to give my publication all the finish I am capable of imparting to it, a few months would suffice to complete it. But as I desire my first attempt to be far above the average, and as I want to be thoroughly conscientious in its preparation, I shall make it my business to undertake a fresh series of researches, which will very likely delay the conclusion of the book for eighteen or twenty months.

My present situation is precarious indeed, but it does support me, or will, as time improves it. The real difficulty does not lie so much in the present as in the future, and the first question I have asked myself has been, "What will this lead to?" People who like to feel their feet at every step they take may think I should be safer if I joined the university at once, even at the risk of vegetating for ever so long in some college. But I do not care to circumscribe the possible area of my life. I desire to leave circumstances and events to play that important part which no human foresight can hope to affect or calculate. Let us allow them to take their natural course, and let us fit ourselves to snatch every opportunity as it arises. The execution of this project would not involve my relinquishing any of our original ones. The École Normale alone would have to be sacrificed. I do not regret that greatly. I have made those inquiries from my former classmate (now a student there) which I mentioned in my last letter, and the result has not proved very enticing. As to my degrees, I am quite determined to carry out that plan. I consider my Bachelor's degree as good as taken. As for my Master's degree, it may be somewhat delayed, but I still hope to be able to get that examination over in the course of the next (scholastic) year. I have always made it a rule of work to have one chief subject of study, and to add to that several secondary subjects to fill up the intervals which must occur in my chief pursuit. After the Master's degree there is nothing but the Doctor's, which is mere child's play, on purely voluntary subjects.

Even supposing the Oriental languages are not destined to become the principal occupation of my life, you will readily understand what inestimable service the fact of my having published a book carrying some weight would do me in any intellectual career. There are numberless positions, the competition for which is decided by an examination of the works published by the candidates. Among these are the university professorships, to which any man holding a Doctor's degree may aspire. As regards the investigations I have to make, my present position affords me every necessary facility.

M. Julien has obtained leave for me to go to the Institute Library and consult the precious MSS. it contains. And a former classmate of mine at St. Sulpice, whose brother is one of the librarians at Ste. Geneviève, has got me permission to *take away* any books I need in *his* name. M. Emmanuel Latouche, whom I have already mentioned, is in charge of the

Semitic Language Department at the Royal Library, and I have no doubt he will be very useful to me. I am carefully attending the lectures my new plan renders necessary to me, amongst others the Arabic course given in connection with the Royal Library and the Collège de France, and I have already come across several useful and pleasant people there. The attendance at these lectures being very small, gives special opportunities of this kind. M. Lelin (of St. Sulpice) had recommended me beforehand to the notice of M. Caussin de Perceval, the Professor of Arabic at the Collège de France, his own old friend and teacher. Lastly, M. Julien seemed very much pleased when I mentioned my idea to him, and has promised me all the hints I need as to the Tartar languages. I constantly see him at the Royal Library, where he spends a great many hours of each day. So, dear sister, my life as regards study is on an excellent footing; and though my future is not quite clear yet, some cheering light is to be seen. Yes, cheering it would be, if only my Henriette would come back to complete my happiness! The activity of the intellectual sphere into which my occupations lead me is very delightful to me. But when I think of the loved one I may never see again, my joy all pales, and life looks sad and dreary. I shall be very happy once hope comes back to me.

I quite forgot to say that if I carry out this new plan I will answer splendidly as a means of making things agreeable to our mother. She believes I am still at the Collège Stanislas; and though my deceit, which amounts to no more than *silence*, is innocent enough, it lies very heavy on my soul. I am certain the new outlook will please her, all the more because the transition from my past life seems so quiet and simple. And it will soon be easy to convince her that my studies and researches made a more independent situation indispensable. She took great pride in the work I had already done in this line, and I am sure she will be delighted.

Dear sister, I have no courage to talk of other things. I can say no more, only repeat the entreaty of my last letter. If you are ill, in God's name tell me so plainly and frankly. And then, Henriette, my beloved! nothing shall keep me back! Not for your sake alone, for mine too, I beseech you! Oh, if my sister should never really know me! Farewell, dearest and best of friends! One word from you will change my sadness to joy and hope. Oh, if I loved you less I should suffer less bitterly! Farewell, dear Henriette!—Your friend,

E. R.

THE END

Recent Biographies.

THE LETTERS OF MATTHEW ARNOLD.
1848–1888.
COLLECTED AND ARRANGED BY GEO. W. E. RUSSELL.
2 vols. 12mo. Cloth. $3.00.

"These two volumes constitute, from the point of view of literature, the most important publications of the season — or, for that matter, of several seasons. The letters are so entirely in accord with the published works that they form a connecting link to bind them together, and they also supply the key to them. As biography, these letters are a great and lasting interest; as literature, they will take their place beside 'Culture and Anarchy,' and 'Essays in Criticism.'" — *The Outlook.*

THE LETTERS OF EDWARD FITZGERALD TO FANNY KEMBLE.
1871–1883.
EDITED BY W. ALDIS WRIGHT, M.A.
2 vols. 12mo. Cloth. $3.00.

"The letters are charming; not too long, almost purely personal, yet not too much so for printing purposes; funny, pathetic, and characteristic." — *Chicago Times-Herald.*

"One of the notable books of the season — so full is the volume of interesting matter and allusion to authors and their work." — *Boston Daily Advertiser.*

LIFE, LETTERS, AND WORKS OF LOUIS AGASSIZ.
By JULES MARCOU.
With Illustrations. 2 vols. 12mo. Cloth. $4.00.

"It is impossible to do justice to this valuable work.... It must suffice to say that the two volumes are exceedingly attractive in their outward form, are profusely illustrated, and will give many hours of pleasure to the reader. In every way, in the matter of style, in the arrangement of incidents, in the impartial criticism of the work of Agassiz, it is altogether charming, and I feel free to assert that it is one of the most delightful biographies I have ever read." — *New York Herald.*

LIFE OF CARDINAL MANNING,
Archbishop of Westminster.
By EDMUND SHERIDAN PURCELL,
MEMBER OF THE ROMAN ACADEMY OF LETTERS.
With Portraits. 2 vols. 8vo. Cloth. $6.00.

"It is a model biography, we had almost said autobiography, for it is largely made up of Manning's letters, extracts from his diaries, journals, and autobiographical notes which he made especially to be used in this work, and all of which he turned over to Mr. Purcell before his death. These rich materials, together with the substance of numerous personal conversations with the Cardinal, have been woven into a sustained narrative by Mr. Purcell, with considerable literary skill and with commendable self-effacement." — *New York Tribune.*

MACMILLAN & CO.,
66 FIFTH AVENUE, NEW YORK.

Recent Biographies.

Baker (Sir Samuel). A Memoir. By T. DOUGLASS MURRAY, F.R.G.S., Executor to the late Samuel Baker, and A. SILVA WHITE, Hon. F.R.S.G.S., author of "The Development of Africa," etc. 8vo. Buckram. $6.00.

The Letters and Literary Remains of Edward Fitzgerald. Edited by WILLIAM ALDIS WRIGHT, M.A. 3 vols. Cloth. $8.00.

The Life and Letters of Edward A. Freeman, D.C.L., LL.D. By W. R. STEPHENS, B.D., Dean of Winchester. 2 vols. 8vo. $7.00.

The Private Life of Warren Hastings, the first Governor-General of India. By Sir CHARLES LAWSON, Fellow of the University of Madras. With Portraits and Illustrations. Demy 8vo. $3.50.

John Knox. A Biography. By P. HUME BROWN, Author of "Life of George Buchanan." In 2 vols. 8vo. Cloth. $7.00.

Recollections of a Happy Life. Being the Autobiography of Marianne North. Edited by her sister, Mrs. JOHN ADDINGTON SYMONDS. With Portraits. 2 vols. $5.00.

Alfred, Lord Tennyson. A Study of His Life and Work. By ARTHUR WAUGH, B.A. Oxon. With Illustrations. 12mo. Cloth. $2.00.

MACMILLAN & CO.,
66 FIFTH AVENUE, NEW YORK.